# Transform
## YOUR STORIES

OVERCOME YOUR TOXIC STORIES, BECOME
A COURAGEOUS AND CONFIDENT LEADER,
AND IMPACT THE WORLD

## *Dedication*

To Mike, the one who keeps me laughing, holds my heart in his hand, and always helps me find the courage I need for the next grand adventure.

*"Man cannot discover new oceans unless he has the courage to lose sight of the shore."*

*- André Gide*

# Contents

Reader Resources ........................................................... 7

Letter to the Reader .................................................. 9

Introduction ................................................................. 11

Chapter 1: Understand Our Stories ....................................... 21

Chapter 2: Discover the Role Stories Play in
     Our Journeys ................................................... 77

Chapter 3: Identify Our Stories .............................................. 95

Chapter 4: Navigate Our Stories ......................................... 123

Chapter 5: Overcome Our Toxic Stories ........................... 149

Final Thoughts ............................................................. 171

Appendix: Transform Our Toxic Team Stories ................. 181

A Grateful Heart ......................................................... 187

About the Author ....................................................... 191

# Reader Resources

One of the primary goals of this book is to help you identify, work through, and transform any toxic stories you've been holding onto in your leadership journey.

Each chapter includes prompts and questions that guide you to capture your thoughts, stories, and reflections.

My hope is that you use this book to work alongside me as I share the struggles my clients and I have faced and worked through so you can overcome your own toxic stories.

To further aid you in this discovery process, I've created some additional reader resources for you, available at www.ashleycox.co/stories.

# Letter to the Reader

Dear Reader,

I had lost my joy.

I looked up one day during a difficult time in my life and realized that I had lost my joy.

What I had been doing wasn't working. What I had thought was my purpose didn't feel aligned. What I had envisioned for my life and business just wasn't coming together.

And the stories I was telling myself about my worth in this world were far from the truth.

Somewhere along the way, I had lost myself.

Gone were the days of being brave, courageous, and bold. The strong, confident, 27-year-old me who had walked into her boss's office one day and asked for—*and gotten!*—a $10,000 raise had faded into just a shell of her former self. She was instead quietly hiding in a corner and encouraging others to go for their dreams and goals, while writing her own off as being unrealistic, unattainable, and, sometimes, downright silly.

Where had she gone? And when? And why?

Then it hit me: She hadn't gone anywhere. She was still me. I was still her.

We were—*and are*—one in the same. But we had lost touch with one another. There's the inner me (the one who whispers quietly inside my head, "You *can* do this," and sometimes screams at me, "*What* are you thinking?! We're gonna get slaughtered!") and the outer me (the me I show to the world).

Have you ever felt that aching disconnect? Have you ever felt that there's something bigger and better for you in this world? That there's a braver, more courageous, and bolder version of you hiding under the surface? That there's a strong and capable leader waiting on the other side of all that fear and doubt?

These insecurities, doubts, and fears are the result of toxic stories in our lives.

One day, we're flying high. On top of the world. Nothing can stop us! And the next? Well, let's just say it's not pretty. Doubting the decisions we make, wondering if we were too harsh in the conversation with an employee, or questioning our career choices (and sanity).

Where did these stories come from? And what can we do about them? That's what we explore together throughout the pages of this book.

I wrote this book for you. For me. For others like us.

In these pages, I share my own personal journey with toxic stories, as well as the journeys of others who've been struggling with them, too. It's real and raw, and I hope you find it relatable. If for no other reason, know that you're not totally and utterly alone in having these stories or feelings—and know that there is hope to overcome them.

The toxic stories never go away completely. We're always coming up with new ones in different situations. But we can learn how to quiet that inner voice that keeps us feeling and playing small. We can step into the person we know we are meant to be—whether that's for the first time or you're ready to connect with the person you used to be again or you're ready for a transformation and a fresh start.

You are so much more than the stories you tell yourself.

— Ashley

# Introduction

*"True leadership stems from individuality that is honestly and sometimes imperfectly expressed. . . . Leaders should strive for authenticity over perfection."*

*- Sheryl Sandberg, COO, Facebook*

Somewhere along the way, you've probably asked yourself, *"Am I really cut out to be a leader?"* or maybe *"Why can't I seem to figure this whole leadership thing out? I must be doing something wrong."* Perhaps you've thought, *"I must have hired all the wrong people. Nothing I do seems to work,"* or even *"Maybe leaders really are born, not made."*

If so, you're in the right place. You see, I wrote this book for you: the leader who's struggling to find her rhythm in her leadership role. The one who is excited and filled with terror at the same time. The one who can't seem to make it all work quite right.

The one with a huge heart, a big dream, and a desire to change the world—but who has no idea how to do that while leading a team and not losing herself.

Being a leader is the most important role you'll ever have in your career. Naturally, it comes with quite a bit of fear and trepidation. Anyone who's ever been in a leadership role will question her abilities at one time or another.

Part of your role as leader is learning how to become the best leader *you* can be—not trying to become someone else or mimic another leader's style. That won't work. You must fully step into your role by leveraging *your* strengths and *your* personality. But if you're dealing with a lot of self-doubt and toxic stories about your abilities, that's hard to do.

A story is an idea we hold about our abilities, skills, knowledge, self-worth, place in this world, or purpose in life. We have some stories that are positive and build us up, that are inspiring and motivating, while other stories are destructive and can wreak havoc in our lives. The latter are what I call toxic stories and they are often formed out of our fears, insecurities, and doubts. In Chapter 1, we'll discuss what stories are in greater detail and I'll share many examples of toxic stories in the coming pages.

*** 

Leaders can be both born *and* made. These are not mutually exclusive ideas. And *all* leaders should continuously work to improve themselves. To become even better versions of themselves over the years.

Since you're reading these words at this very moment in time, I imagine you feel somewhat the same way. You might be tired of what's not working and are ready for a change. Or perhaps you're dealing with some self-doubt that's been coming up for you in your leadership role. Maybe you're worried about stepping into a leadership role because you're unsure whether or not you'll be a good leader.

Regardless of your reason for being here, one thing is for sure: You don't want to be a horrible boss—one whom employees don't respect, complain about, are fearful of, don't give their best effort to, and won't stick around for the long haul.

Even the greatest leaders face fear, uncertainty, and doubt about their abilities. They tell themselves stories about what they can and can't do that aren't true, borne of experiences they've had in the past and that continue to be perpetuated through the lens of their beliefs.

These false stories we tell and believe about ourselves can have damaging side effects on our self-esteem, self-worth, relationships, and professional lives.

The difference is, exceptional leaders know that they occasionally hold onto stories about their abilities that aren't true. And they work through them so they can become stronger, more capable leaders who earn the trust and respect of their teams.

Once you see how these toxic stories play out in daily life, it's much easier to identify your own, both personally and in your leadership journey, that are holding you back. Here's a simple example of some typical events that can occur in a day.

Imagine you are getting ready to head out of the house to work at your local coffee shop for the day. You wanted to be at the coffee shop, tapping away at your keyboard, at 8 a.m. sharp. Unfortunately, you're running late. As you rush around throwing on clothes you slam your toe into the foot of your bedpost and think, *"Oh shit! So, it's going to be one of those days. Sigh."*

You immediately form a toxic story in your mind (today is going to be a bad day) based on these seemingly unrelated—and normal—occurrences (you're running late and you stubbed your toe).

You finally get yourself together and out the door. On your drive to the coffee shop you hit every single red light in town. The story continues, *"Ugh, see?! I just can't believe this. Of course I hit every light in town when I'm already late. This is not a great start to the day."*

You continue on and finally arrive at the coffee shop at 8:45 a.m.—45 minutes later than you had planned. Upon placing your order, the barista (who can sense your frustrated vibe) nervously tells you that they're out of caramel syrup for your caramel macchiato and asks what you'd like instead. You snap back, *"Of course you are! Why would you have caramel syrup today, of all days? I should have just stayed home."* Your toxic story is now not only impacting you, but spilling over into someone else's day.

You order a vanilla latte instead and finally sit down at a table to work, thinking to yourself, *"This whole day is a nightmare. I just want to go back home, put on my PJs and crawl into bed, and forget it ever happened. I'm never coming out to work at a coffee shop again!"*

Have you ever had one of those days? I know I have. One seemingly small inconvenience suddenly snowballs into another and another and another. Before you know it, you're feeling the same way as the woman in this example.

Here's the thing, though: Sometimes these minor inconveniences can actually be positives. We just don't know it at the time. Maybe the woman in our example stubbed her toe so she would leave the house late, avoiding a nasty accident on the highway. Perhaps she hit every red light in town because an animal was darting across the road and she would have swerved to miss it, only to end up in the ditch with thousands of dollars in damage to her car. Consider that the coffee shop was out of caramel syrup because it was contaminated with E. coli, but no one had discovered that yet, and she could have ended up very ill from her drink. Or maybe they were all just minor nuisances that came up in her day because life doesn't always go smoothly.

We may never know. What we can do is choose to look at these situations from a different angle. Sometimes these inconveniences aren't meant to ruffle our feathers. They're meant to keep us safe, to protect us, and to make sure we don't end up somewhere we're not supposed to be. The same can be said of the stories we believe about our ability to lead.

It's easy to look at situations and get frustrated, irritated, and overwhelmed by them. I encourage you to look at them as bumper guards in the game of life, meant to keep you safe and in your lane.

However, when we refuse to see the beauty in the day, we are adding to the story we're already telling ourselves.

» Stubbed toe = bad day.
» Caught every red light in town = confirms bad day.
» Out of caramel syrup at coffee shop = further confirms bad day.

When one bad thing happens, we have a heightened awareness to continue seeing every little inconvenience as further proof to support our story. What if we were so busy paying attention to the bad that we failed to see or notice all the good? Like the impromptu breakfast you had with your spouse that initially caused your delay, the sweet snuggles with your pup before heading out the door, the fact that someone was kind in traffic and immediately let you over when a lane was blocked, or that nice lady in line behind you at the coffee shop who paid you a compliment right before you placed your order.

So much of life—and consequently our leadership journeys—has to do with perspective and the stories we tell ourselves. We so often see one bad or unfortunate thing as negative, which can easily spiral into multiple things viewed as negative. We're looking for things to support our theory that *"Today is going to be a bad day."* And when we do that, you better believe we're going to find them every single time.

You might have done one Facebook Live on your business page that got 35 views. Your story immediately becomes *"See, no one is interested in what I have to say! I'm not going to do this again. It's not worth my time."* But my friend, *35 people* watched your first Live. That's nothing to be ashamed about. Those are 35 lives you impacted just from doing one short live video on a social media platform. Building up viewership takes time and consistency. People have to know you're doing them before they can watch them. Then, they need to know you're doing them consistently—that you're showing up for them on a regular basis. When you stop before you even get started, you're doing yourself (and your audience) a disservice.

The same is true for our leadership journeys. A story I hear quite frequently from my clients is *"Maybe I'm just not cut out to be a leader."* Why do you believe this to be true? Because you've never been a leader before? Because it's intimidating and you're worried you're going to mess something up? Because you don't know what you're doing?

At various points in your life, you didn't know how to drive a car, tie your shoes, walk, or even feed yourself. But with time, practice, and positive reinforcement from those who loved you, you learned these important life skills and (hopefully) became quite good at them.

As I alluded to earlier, perhaps you've heard the saying *Leaders are born, not made.* I don't buy into this philosophy. I think leaders can be both born *and* made. I can clearly see this in my own leadership journey. Over the years, I've taken many personality assessments. As an independence-loving free spirit, most assessments say that someone with my personality type typically doesn't enjoy being in a leadership role because of the demands of the position. Being in a leadership role can often feel too demanding and restrictive—almost suffocating.

However, knowing my personality type, and what I enjoy and don't enjoy, I've learned how to lead in a way that feels really good to me. I focus on developing teams that are self-sufficient problem-solvers and that don't have to rely on me for every little thing. This, in turn, creates stronger, more capable teams and gives me the freedom I not only crave, but need. Knowing more about myself and how I show up in this world has helped me to become a better, more effective leader, while enjoying the role (and my freedom) greatly.

The same can be true for you. But first, you have to stop telling yourself that leaders are born, not made, or that you're not cut out to be a leader. These toxic stories are holding you back from becoming the best leader you can be.

The greatest leaders of all time, who many believe were born to be great leaders, have also had a strong focus on continuous learning. They constantly seek to improve their skills on their leadership journeys, because they know there is always more to learn in order to improve. They've made plenty of their own mistakes and have certainly had their fair share of forehead-slapping moments of embarrassment and regret—but they didn't allow these imperfect moments of their leadership journeys to hold them back from learning and doing better.

Leadership doesn't just happen because a new title is bestowed upon you, whether by someone at the company you work for or when you hire your first employee in your own business. You develop into a leader through study, experience, practice, and, yes, making plenty of mistakes along the way.

A great leader knows that her leadership training is never complete. She spends time with other leaders, seeking advice, getting constructive feedback, and challenging her own beliefs and practices. Great leaders know they don't know everything. They're open and willing to try new things, because they know doing so will only make them stronger in the end. Great leaders are invested in their own growth, because they know that it ultimately benefits their teams, and their teams deserve for them to be their best.

Once you stop thinking of being a leader as the destination, and more like the journey that it is, you'll be able to release some of the pressure, worry, and doubts you've been carrying around with you and become a stronger, more confident leader for your team and yourself.

As the old Chinese proverb says, "*The best time to plant a tree was 20 years ago. The second best time is now.*" The best time to start your leadership journey is today, not in six months, in five years, or 20 years down the road. Whether you have a team right now or not, you can start building your leadership muscles. If you start today, think of where you'll be by the time those months and years roll around. Imagine the lives you will have impacted by stepping into your leadership role sooner, committing to your own self-development, and being courageous enough to face your own insecurities and doubts.

In the coming pages, we explore one aspect of leadership that gets in the way of truly becoming the best leaders we can be: the toxic stories we tell ourselves and believe as truths. We not only going to dive deep into what these are, where they come from, and why we have them, but we learn how to recognize them when we feel them coming on, to call them out for what they really are, and to overcome them one by one.

I share insights about toxic stories that I've learned from my work as a leader, as well as from training and mentoring other leaders over the past 13 years. But this isn't going to be a one-sided journey. I've crafted exercises and Journal

Prompts to help aid you in uncovering, navigating, and overcoming your own toxic stories.

One goal that was of utmost importance to me as I conceptualized and wrote this book was to be able to walk alongside you for the journey. I provide you with plenty of white space to journal, take notes, explore thoughts and ideas, reflect on past experiences, and work through your own toxic stories alongside me.

So get messy. Write your heart out. Dig deep into those toxic stories you've been holding onto, so that you can let them go and become the confident and courageous leader you dream of being.

Are you ready? Let's dive in!

# *Chapter 1*
# Understand Our Stories

*"Courage starts with showing up and letting ourselves be seen."*

*- Brené Brown,* Daring Greatly

First, and most importantly, begin by understanding exactly what I mean when I say "stories we tell ourselves." In this chapter, we explore what stories are, the different types of stories we can have (*spoiler alert*: There are two primary types of stories: healthy and toxic), who struggles with toxic stories, where they come from, and how and when they show up in our lives.

But first, a short story to get us started.

I love true crime podcasts. It's my favorite podcast genre. One sunny afternoon, when I was taking a mid-afternoon break, I was listening to the true crime podcast *Someone Knows Something,* by CBC Radio in Canada.

Narrator David Ridgen, an investigative journalist, host, and director, was weaving a captivating story of the events that transpired in a 40-year-old cold case of a five-year-old boy, Adrien McNaughton, who had been last seen during a summer fishing trip with his family near his home in eastern Ontario, Canada.

Haunted, sad, and puzzled (the boy vanished without a trace), I was listening intently when a phrase unexpectedly snatched my attention away from the story that was unfolding.

*"It's easier to believe the narrative you want than the truth you're in."*

I paused the episode to jot down this sentence. I read it and re-read it for a while, turning it over in my mind. *It's easier to believe the narrative you want than the truth you're in.*

In the episode, David was talking about how investigators, detectives, and cops develop theories about how a crime likely occurred, and who was involved, by gathering and reviewing available evidence. As they look at sometimes seemingly unrelated pieces of evidence, they try to make sense of it all and begin to craft narratives—or stories—to explain what might have happened. Occasionally, they're so committed to one specific story they start to unintentionally look for evidence to further support it.

This occurrence is called *confirmation bias.* According to Shahram Heshmat, writing for *Psychology Today* in April 2015, "Confirmation bias occurs from the direct influence of desire on beliefs. . . . Once we have formed a view, we embrace information that confirms that view while ignoring, or rejecting, information that casts doubt on it. Confirmation bias suggests we don't perceive circumstances objectively."

Someone might even get so wrapped up in the story they've been crafting that they overlook or even ignore other critical pieces of information that don't support their story. This overlooked information might tell a more accurate story, which could lead to breakthroughs in the case or the capture of the offender.

As with most things in life, our circumstances can affect how we respond. Confirmation bias is often stronger in emotionally charged situations and those when deeply held beliefs are involved (like in the case of a missing five-year-old boy who disappeared without a single shred of evidence), meaning there is more room for ignoring or rejecting information to the contrary.

What does this have to do with you and your leadership journey?

We can learn lessons from all areas of our lives if we're paying attention. This just happens to be one of those times and one of those unlikely places.

As I thought about this phrase that had snagged my attention, our tendency to form stories about our leadership journeys hit me.

I explored the topic some more and decided to write a blog post about my thoughts. That post turned into a short series of blog posts—and finally into the pages of the book you're reading right now.

If you think back to the story I shared in the chapter opening, you can see confirmation bias at play. A couple of small irritations (the stubbed toe and running late) became a "bad day." From there, other "negative" things that were happening throughout the day (hitting every red light and no caramel syrup for the coffee) only served to reinforce the story that this was a bad day. Yet, all the good that happened was overlooked (the impromptu breakfast with the spouse, snuggles with the pup, the kind person in traffic, and the compliment from the stranger in line).

Sometimes, we have healthy stories that bolster our confidence and allow us to show up in big ways in our lives and businesses. Other times, we craft toxic stories that don't show the whole picture or that can put a negative spin on an entire situation, day, week, month, year, or even lifetime. These toxic stories keep us from living our best lives, appreciating the good things in this world, and reaching our fullest potential.

The stories we tell ourselves over time become a part of us, if we allow them. I could see this playing out in my own life. Why had I never become the singer I always longed to be? Because I told myself stories that I wasn't good enough, wasn't talented enough, and didn't have the right connections. I allowed those stories to hold me back from even trying. And sadly, that's our greatest failure of all: not even trying at all. I let something I loved doing—something that gave me so much joy and life—slowly die because of the toxic stories I told myself. Imagine what life would be like if that wasn't the case—if I had chosen not to believe those lies and had taken action instead.

Throughout this book, we not only discuss what stories are and where they come from, but we also explore your own toxic stories that might be holding you back and take action on clearing out those old, unhelpful stories—to make room for newer, more positive and healthy stories that will help you become the leader you want and need to be.

## What Are Stories?

A story is an idea we hold about our abilities, skills, knowledge, self-worth, place in this world, or purpose in life. We craft stories about our ability to run a business, climb the corporate ladder, raise children, be a good spouse or friend, speak in public, be an advocate, perform our craft or profession, and so much more. We craft these stories about nearly everything we are, do, or want to do in life.

Our minds are constantly trying to assess and make sense of what's going on. One of the ways it does this is to take all of the data points of the situation we're facing and then use reasoning, based on knowledge and past experiences, to develop a story about the situation and to protect us from the situation, if it assesses it to be potentially dangerous.

Some stories are positive and build us up. They give us courage and drive us forward. They're inspiring and they motivate us. Other stories are damaging and can wreak havoc in our lives, both personally and professionally, or hold us back from reaching our full potential.

Some stories are founded in the truth; we concoct other stories based upon our fears, insecurities, and doubts. When we allow ourselves to live inside false stories for too long, those untruths start to become true for us.

I believe—and I've shared this with the many leaders I've mentored over the years—that our employees will either live up to, or down to, our expectations of them. When we have high expectations for our teams, they will more often than not rise to the occasion. However, when we expect little of them, they will never strive to do more than what we expect. In other words, they are living down to our low expectations. High performers will continue to work in a high-performing mode, but it's likely to be in another business (*aka* they quit and go work somewhere else). We can impact this because we're the one creating the stories about our team's capabilities.

## Setting Expectations

Just like the stories we tell ourselves regarding our ability to lead a team, our team stories can be just as, if not more, damaging.

A saying that I've used for years and have shared with countless leaders throughout my career is "People will live up to, or down to, your expectations of them. What kind of expectations are you setting?"

It's a similar sentiment to what Stephen R. Covey wrote in his acclaimed book *The 7 Habits of Highly Effective People*: "Treat a man as he is and he will remain as he is. Treat a man as he can and should be and he will become as he can and should be."

When we set the bar low, people don't have a lot to work toward or achieve. It's demotivating and often demeaning. And it's almost like giving them a free pass to just coast. But here's the thing: Most people don't want to "just coast."

Meaningful work is the single largest contributor to a positive employee experience, according to a study by Globoforce titled "Employee Experience around the Globe." Sadly, only one out of every 10 employees said their overall work experience has significantly exceeded their expectations, according to Alight's 2018 Workforce Mindset Study—which means there's *a lot* of room for improvement!

People want to make a difference, be a contributing and valued member of a team, and do meaningful work. As leaders, we must understand what our employees want, need, and expect—and then do our best to provide those.

The same is true for us: We either live up to the positive expectations and stories we tell ourselves, or live down to those that are negative, toxic, and destructive.

A story is something we usually tell ourselves, subconsciously, with very little effort or thought going into it. Oftentimes, we find ourselves in the midst of a story and we don't even know how we got there. We craft some stories over the course of our lifetime, adding new chapters and plot twists along the way. You've probably heard someone say, *"If you don't like the part of the story you're in, just wait because you'll find yourself in a new chapter soon,"* right? Well, I don't want to wish my life away, waiting to turn the pages until I reach the next chapter, and I'm betting that you don't either.

We all have a mix of both healthy and toxic stories, which we'll discuss in more detail over the coming pages. There are parts of our lives in which we feel confident and in control, and other parts in which we feel insecure and fearful. It's just human nature.

However, it's important that we recognize the stories we tell ourselves each and every day, so we can actively work to change them if they don't support our dreams, goals, and desires.

At the end of the day, we all have the ability to change our stories. And that's pretty damn empowering!

## Healthy Stories

Healthy stories are exactly what they sound like: *healthy!*

These are stories we tell ourselves that are good for us and for those around us. They build up our confidence, give us the courage to go bigger and bolder in life and business, and allow us to truly show up as the best versions of ourselves in the world.

Healthy stories are identified by positive character traits, such as confidence, courage, integrity, honesty, kindness, persistence, and fairness.

Healthy stories have no place for arrogance, manipulative or controlling behaviors, getting defensive or angry, or showing up dishonesty, disrespectfully, or with rudeness.

It's important to note that an individual with an "overly healthy" sense of self is not embodying healthy stories. This person is usually struggling with some very intense and strongly held toxic stories that are being masked by seemingly positive traits.

## Toxic Stories

We have the opportunity to craft a new, more compelling, and impactful story. In this book, we explore the various stories we tell ourselves, both personally and professionally, with a specific focus on the ones that particularly impact our leadership journey.

The stories we tell ourselves can sometimes be positive ones, like my client who said, *"In my corporate job, I was a great leader. I was the best, actually!"* She went on to say that she was great at giving her team encouragement and solid feedback, that she wasn't a pushover but also remained flexible, and that she loved to partner with her HR team. But as she began to talk about her journey into business ownership, she shared that she had gotten "rusty." She needed some guidance on how to delegate things to her team without overwhelming them, and how to motivate her team and get them excited about building and growing this business with her. She said to me, *"I need to get better at managing my team. I know this comes from owning my own business and not working for someone else. I have insecurities about my business and I don't want to show those to my team."*

Her ability to lead didn't vanish like a thief in the night—it's still there—but the stories she is telling herself have changed. When she was in a corporate position, she didn't have the fears, doubts, and insecurities about owning and running her own business. If you own a business, you know these are aplenty. Constant worries about whether it will be a raging success or a massive failure. Knowing that if it all comes crumbling down, it would be all her fault. And no matter how wonderful a leader she was to her team, they would all be out of jobs because of her. No pressure, right?!

Her fears and doubts about her ability to lead her team weren't even really about leading her team. They stemmed from her preconceived notions about her ability to successfully run a business, without the support of a large company behind her. The interesting thing is that those worries spilled over into her ability to lead (and very likely other areas of her life she wasn't even quite aware of). She wasn't able to give her team her best and show up for them in the ways she was used to, because she was weaving in toxic stories about whether or not she was going to be a good business owner and whether she even had what it takes.

Let's dig a little deeper here and explore the effects this has on a team. When a leader doesn't believe in her own abilities, how do you think that impacts her team? Each and every team member feeds off of the energy the leader puts out into the world as a leader. They watch every move the leader makes and listen to each word she shares. When a leader's energy and actions don't align, team members are the first to know it.

A leader who tries to show up as always being confident—saying and doing all the "right" things," but putting an energy or vibration out into the world that's shrouded in negativity, doubt, and fear—has a team that will notice. They're going to talk about it. Worry about it. Stress about it. And then their work is going to be impacted. They may even get the nagging sense things aren't going very well and it might be time to jump ship.

Here's something important to remember: As leaders, we are still human.

We're allowed to worry and stress and doubt ourselves. But the more a leader tries to hide it from their team, the more they're going to call bullshit. Everything else we try to do is going to come into question. When trust is broken within a team, it's hard as hell to restore. (It can be done, but it will take far more effort to earn it back than if we worked to keep it in the first place.)

Of course, there has to be some balance here. As a leader, it's best not to share every single worry, fear, and doubt with our team, but it's okay to share that we're facing those things and working through them. While we don't want to scare them, we want to be open, honest, and vulnerable with our team—to show them that we're human and have human experiences just like they do. This in turn allows them to be human and have human experiences with us, creating a connection that goes far beyond employer and employee. Being human with your team builds credibility, trust, and respect.

For the purposes of this book, we focus on exploring toxic stories in depth. Throughout the coming pages, I encourage you to look within. Be open and honest with yourself about what toxic stories you have been holding onto and how they are impacting your life and your role as a leader. Every word in this book was written with you in mind.

## Toxic Stories vs. Negative Self-Talk

At first consideration, toxic stories and negative self-talk might seem like one in the same, when in fact, they are not.

A toxic story is a full-fledged story we tell ourselves about a particular situation or event in our lives. Negative self-talk is how that story then shows up in day-to-day life and how we reaffirm that story in the words and language that we use. Recall when we talked about how we look for ways to confirm our beliefs earlier. Negative self-talk is a way that we confirm those beliefs through our own spoken word. The more we tell ourselves these stories, the more we—and those around us—believe them. That then gives us more evidence that this story is in fact true, because others start to look for situations and events to confirm our toxic story.

A friend was having a particularly challenging time in her marriage. She had been arguing with her husband for weeks and they'd . . . well, let's just say they'd lost that lovin' feeling. She started to convince herself that he didn't care about her and that he wasn't even trying anymore. In fact, she was dead certain he was doing everything in his power to annoy her and just be an ass in general. For example, he:

» Forgot to get milk from the store on his way home from work.
» Left his dirty clothes on the bathroom floor.
» Didn't wipe the counter after fixing the baby's bottle.
» Failed to call when he had to work late unexpectedly.

If she could come up with one example of how her husband simply didn't care anymore, she could come up with a thousand. But honestly, if you've been married any time at all, you know how easy it is to fall into this trap of every single little thing becoming evidence used against the offending party, right?

When she would tell me about his latest offense, she would use words and phrases like:

» *He just doesn't care about me anymore.*
» *I don't think he loves me. Just* listen *to what he did now.*
» *All he cares about is work, work, work.*
» *I think he's doing this on purpose just to get on my nerves.*

She collected all of these little "offenses" to use as ammunition against him. She started to form the story that he didn't love her anymore with a handful of little incidents over the course of a particularly hard week. Then she started to reaffirm the toxic story she believed by associating every offense afterward with the story of "he doesn't love me anymore." The more she used this negative self-talk to cement these stories in her own mind (as well as try to get her friends to agree with her), the more they built momentum and started to stick.

As I'm sure you can imagine, the situation started to spiral out of hand pretty quickly. The more she bought into the story she was telling herself, the more she and her husband started pulling apart. She would tell me things like "He says I'm being ridiculous for feeling this way," which, of course, fired her up even more and gave her yet another thing to add to her laundry list of offenses.

As her friend, and someone on the outside of the situation, I could easily see what was going on, even though I didn't know her husband's side of the story. With two small kids in the mix, things were chaotic and busy. They were both tired and frustrated and were lashing out at one another, as you do when you live in close quarters with another human being with the weight of your responsibilities hanging between you constantly.

As she was telling me about her husband's blatant offenses day after day and sharing her negative self-talk, I started to ask some questions to get her to think through things a bit more:

>> Why do you think he's doing these things on purpose?
>> Has he ever left his dirty clothes on the bathroom floor before?
>> Does he make it a habit of working late all the time and not calling?

In other words, I encouraged her to challenge these assumptions she had and to look at her relationship from a more objective stance. She was stuck in this downward spiral of feeling unappreciated, couldn't communicate it well with her husband, and then lashed out at him for any and every little "sin" he committed. This approach wasn't getting her anywhere. It wasn't getting *them* anywhere. She was gradually getting more and more frustrated and desperate. And I'm sure he was feeling it, too.

Once she started looking at the truth of her relationship (and the current situation she had found herself in) through an objective lens, she was soon able to realize that these offenses weren't intentional. They were normal behaviors: a human being human, accidents and mistakes being made, and best efforts being given.

She was able to take a look at her relationship with a fresh perspective and see all the ways her husband was showing up for her—and, yes, still loving her, even on the really hard days. She was also able to look at the role she was playing in their relationship, good as well as unhelpful.

Sometimes, it takes someone outside of our own heads to call us out on our bullshit. To ask us the hard questions about the situation and our role in it. And to love us through our craziness. Because that's exactly what these toxic stories become: craziness.

*Journal Prompt: As you go begin this journey with me of uncovering and overcoming the toxic stories that are holding you back from reaching your full potential, let's begin with our first journal prompt. Keep these questions (and your answers) in mind as you read this book.*

*There are additional resources to help aid you in the journaling and overcome your toxic stories. You can access and download these at www.ashleycox.co/stories.*

*Who's the greatest leader you've ever worked for or with?*

_____

_____

*What characteristics or traits made this leader so great?*

_____

_____

_____

_____

*What flaws did this leader have or what mistakes did they make?*

_____

_____

_____

_____

*Did the flaws of this leader make them any less great in your eyes? Why or why not?*

_____

_____

_____

_____

*Now, think about your own flaws. Why would these hold you back from being a great leader?*

_____

_____

_____

_____

_____

_____

*What strengths do you embody that could aid you in your leadership journey?*

_____

_____

_____

_____

_____

_____

*Have you ever known someone who wasn't perfect, but whom you admire anyway? Write about that individual here. What made them great? Why did their flaws not matter?*

_____

_____

_____

_____

_____

_____

_____

*Write about someone who has shared their own toxic stories with you here. Who is this person? What is their relationship to you? Did you think any less of them because of these stories they shared with you? What did you say to this person when they shared their insecurities, fears, and doubts with you—the toxic stories running through their mind?*

_____

_____

_____

_____

_____

## Who Struggles with Toxic Stories?

Think you're the only leader who has ever doubted herself? Think again, sister! Nearly every human on this planet has struggled with toxic stories at one point or another. Some people are more naturally inclined to go immediately to the worst-case scenario, while others have a generally more optimistic or positive outlook on life. And others still seem like they have it all together on the outside, and might even come off as being so confident that they're arrogant, yet they face the same dilemma the rest of us do with these negative stories. They just have a tendency to hide them from the rest of us.

To illustrate that we *all* struggle with toxic stories throughout our lives, let's look at some toxic stories from a variety of people from many different backgrounds: famous people, successful clients I've worked with, and a few of my own.

It's hard to imagine a Pulitzer Prize–winning author having any sort of toxic stories, isn't it? But that's exactly what happened to John Steinbeck, who struggled with imposter syndrome. The website Open Culture reported that Steinbeck wrote in a 1938 journal, "I am not a writer. I've been fooling myself and other people." Wow, how many times have you felt that way? I know I have, especially when I took on higher-level positions in my corporate career and when I started my first business. In the late 1930s, while working on his famous novel *The Grapes of Wrath,* Steinbeck also wrote: "I am assailed by my own ignorance and inability. . . . Sometimes, I seem to do a little good piece of work, but when it is done it slides into mediocrity." Considering that this book helped land him the Pulitzer Prize in 1962, I don't think Steinbeck gave himself enough credit for the work he did.

Sometimes, our greatest insecurities and biggest self-doubts hold us back from achieving our greatest works. I can only imagine what Steinbeck's inner voice was saying, but it was likely stories such as:

> » *Who do you think you are to write a book?*
> » *This is garbage. No one's going to read this!*
> » *If you publish this book, what will your friends and family think?*
> » *You'll be ridiculed when people start reading your book.*
> » *You should just quit now and save yourself the humiliation.*

What if Steinbeck had bought into those stories and never completed *The Grapes of Wrath?* We wouldn't have one of the greatest novels ever written—and he wouldn't have won the Pulitzer Prize. Here's a tip: If the toxic stories are getting louder or stronger or more present, it probably means you're on to something really, really good. So don't put aside what you're working on until it's finished!

Many times, you hear stories about struggling artists who would give up anything just to keep doing the thing they love. And you hear about the toxic stories they tell themselves about their circumstances and how their work is never good enough. That's why we still find old sketches and starts of projects from famous artists many years after their deaths.

When Pope Julius II asked Michelangelo to paint the ceiling of the Vatican's Sistine Chapel, Michelangelo refused, saying he was a sculptor, not a painter. As you know, he eventually relented. He spent the next four years creating a masterpiece that millions of people visit every year—more than 500 years later.

Obviously, we know he was telling himself a story by saying he was a sculptor, not a painter, but let's consider what else he might have been thinking:

- » *Why on earth would anyone ask me, of all people, to take on this huge project?*
- » *Sure, I dabble in painting, but I'm not very good at it.*
- » *There are many other, far more talented painters in the world.*
- » *What if I do this project and it turns out horribly? I'll be the laughingstock of the city!*

Isn't it humbling to think that one of the greatest painters who ever lived likely had these, and many other, similar, thoughts racing through his mind regarding one of his life's greatest works? Had Michelangelo succumbed to those thoughts, we wouldn't have the breathtaking art of the Sistine Chapel.

Now, imagine being a woman in the 1800s—a woman who wanted to be taken seriously as an author during that time period. Not only are you struggling with self-doubts and toxic stories about your craft, but you're also facing scrutiny as a female author. That's exactly what happened to George Eliot, of Middlemarch fame, *aka* Mary Anne Evans. She was so worried that her writing wouldn't be taken seriously because she was stepping outside of the traditional, light-hearted romance genres ladies were expected to be writing about that time and into a world of realism and psychological insight. And she adopted a pen name in order to do it. I can almost feel the thoughts that must have overwhelmed her at times:

- » *A woman has never written this kind of book before. Who am I to write it?*
- » *What if someone discovers that George Eliot is a woman—and that woman is me? I'll be mortified!*
- » *I know I won't be able to write like a man. Surely they'll figure that out it right away.*

> » *What if everyone laughs at my book when it's published?*
> » *Maybe I should just stick to writing what women are supposed to write about.*

Mary Anne Evans was willing to fight her own inner demons and push through the toxic stories she was telling herself, and she opened up a new world of opportunities for female authors who came after. Her bravery not only changed her life, but the lives of all those behind her. Maybe I wouldn't be sitting here writing this book for you, if it hadn't been for her.

Many examples exist of one person overcoming their toxic stories to impact the world on a greater scale. Take Dr. Martin Luther King, Jr., for instance. Even the charismatic and confident leader of the civil rights movement struggled with fear, despair, and self-doubt. Any number of things could have easily stopped him (or anyone in his position) in his tracks. We know he struggled with these things because he shared them. At one point, Dr. King admitted that decided to back quietly out of a protest, describing the moment with this sentiment: "It seemed that all my fears had come down on me at once. . . . And I got to the point that I couldn't take it any longer. I was weak." It's easy to imagine the many stories he told himself during his lifetime:

> » *I'm not sure I can do this. There has to be someone better suited to lead the way.*
> » *Who do I think I am for going up against the president of the United States?*
> » *What if no one takes me seriously? My message will probably fall on deaf ears.*
> » *Nothing I do is ever enough. Maybe I should quit before things get worse.*

Every time Dr. King stepped up to the podium to give a speech, he faced not only criticism, but downright hatred. During his lifetime, he was one of the most hated people in America. And yet, he persevered with his message and his mission because he was keenly aware that the work he was doing was far more important than his reputation—that it would change lives. If not him, then who would step up to lead this change? His mission was greater than his fears and doubts, so he continued to do the work he was called to do— an important lesson for us all.

Finally, let's talk about another prominent leader who has struggled with her own toxic stories: Sheryl Sandberg, COO of Facebook and author of *Lean In: Women, Work and the Will to Lead*. In a *Woman & Home* (February 2018) article, she shared her top tips for having more confidence. Here's one tip she shared: "I still sometimes find myself spoken over and discounted while men sitting next to me are not. But now I know how to take a deep breath and keep my hand up. I have learned to sit at the table."

We know, from her own admission, that Sandberg has felt less than and like a fraud. Some other thoughts she may have had running through her mind at one time might sound like this:

> » *I'm the only woman in the room. No one is going to listen to any of my ideas.*
> » *What if I make a mistake and everyone finds out I'm a fraud?*
> » *I have to act like someone else in order to sit at this table. I certainly can't be myself.*
> » *What if I don't have all the skills I need? I won't be able to do this job.*

The stories of famous people, of historical figures, and of everyday individuals who have struggled with self-doubt, toxic narratives, fear, and uncertainty are as plentiful as there are people on this earth. If you've been alive, you've likely faced some sort of toxic narrative in your lifetime. They're not only present in our work, our businesses, and our leadership roles, they're present in our relationships with our spouses, in our parenting, and even in our hobbies. They show up at different times, in different capacities, and in different ways. But they're always there, lingering under the surface. Watching and waiting to come up and pull us down into the murky mire of "not good enough-ness" and keeping us from reaching our full potential.

But what about the everyday person? What about the toxic stories that women in business face each day? Here are some stories that you might find yourself nodding along to:

» A woman who shared on Instagram about a new co-working space she was trying and whispered into the camera, "I kinda don't feel cool enough to be here. These people are *so* cool!!"

» A woman who timidly posted in a Facebook group that she was "not sure what to post about [her business] online. I don't have anything interesting to say."

» A woman who shared, "I fear I will die with all of my dreams and hidden potential locked inside me."

» A woman who was convinced she'd never succeed because "I suck at selling."

» A woman drowning in work because "I'm the worst at delegating because I want to control every detail."

» A woman whose inner voice is screaming, "Get it together!!" which only results in more shame when she can't seem to get it together.

> » A woman who candidly shared, "Every time I succeed, I chalk it up to luck or fraud."
>
> » A woman who said, "I can't help it, but every time I post on social media, I obsessively check to see how many likes and comments my post got. When I don't get what I consider a 'good response,' I get depressed because I feel like no one cares."
>
> » The woman who struggles with feeling worthy of earning more money who shared, "My inner voice says, 'You are not worthy of receiving more. Don't get greedy.'"

Do any of these resonate with you? I believe that we've all faced similar stories at some point.

The following set of prompts is designed to get your thinking deeply about your own personal toxic stories. I won't lie to you and tell you it will be easy. It will take some deep self-awareness and reflection, as well as some time to get through this section. Don't shy away from this exercise, though, because it might be difficult or uneasy. Lean into it for those exact reasons. When we dig in and do the deep work, we make better progress faster, and we avoid falling victim to the same toxic stories again in the future. Studies and research have shown that self-awareness is one of the most important traits a successful leader can have. Know that the work you do in this prompt (as well as throughout this book) will help you develop one of the most vitally important skills in your leadership journey.

*Journal Prompt:* *What toxic stories have you been telling yourself about your relationship with your:*

*Parents?*

_____
_____
_____
_____
_____

*Spouse/Significant Other?*

_____
_____
_____
_____
_____

*Children?*

_____
_____
_____
_____
_____

*Friends?*

_____
_____
_____
_____
_____

*Leader/Boss/Supervisor?*

_____
_____
_____
_____
_____

*Coworkers/Colleagues?*

_____

_____

_____

_____

_____

_____

*Employees/Direct Reports?*

_____

_____

_____

_____

_____

*Now, think about the role you play in various areas of your life. What toxic stories are you telling yourself about your role as a/an:*

*Child?*

_____

_____

_____

_____

*Spouse/Significant Other?*

_____

_____

_____

_____

_____

*Parent?*

_____
_____
_____
_____
_____

*Friend?*

_____
_____
_____
_____
_____

*Employee?*

_____
_____
_____
_____
_____

*Coworker/Colleague?*

_____
_____
_____
_____
_____

*Leader/Boss/Supervisor?*

_____
_____
_____
_____
_____

*Volunteer/Advocate?*

_____

_____

_____

_____

_____

*Community Member?*

_____

_____

_____

_____

_____

*Human Being with Hobbies, Passions, and Goals Outside of Work and Family?*

_____

_____

_____

_____

_____

*Do you notice any themes arising from your reflections on these specific relationships and roles in your life? What are they?*

_____

_____

_____

_____

_____

*Do your toxic stories seem to be louder or more prominent at certain times than others? When?*

_____

_____

_____

_____

_____

*What triggers these toxic stories to form (stress, a new situation,*
*something your parent/spouse/child/boss says or does, etc.)?*

_____

_____

_____

_____

_____

The first step in being able to overcome the powerful toxic stories we tell ourselves is being aware of them, then understanding where they're coming from and writing them down. Without properly recognizing our toxic stories, they continue to eat at us from the inside out—a slow, debilitating, and agonizing gnawing from within. By exploring the toxic stories we hold in various areas of our personal and professional lives, we're able to see patterns of belief we have that lead to patterns of behavior that aren't serving us.

Like a child who's afraid of the monster under the bed, we have to turn on the light to see that there's actually nothing there to be afraid of—except the fear of the unknown. Turn on the light, look under the bed, and call out your monsters.

Remember: These toxic stories don't usually jump out from under the bed and roar in your face unexpectedly. They're the whispers that breeze through your mind from the quiet recesses of the room.

Allow me to share a quick example I had with my own monsters not too long ago. Every day, I receive HARO (Help a Reporter Out) emails, which connect people looking for opportunities to share their knowledge and expertise through various platforms with the journalists seeking those sources to use for quotes and stories in their articles, blogs, and podcasts. Even though I've been getting and responding to these requests for a couple of years now, sometimes I still struggle with feeling good enough, smart enough, articulate enough, just *enough,* when the requests pop into my in-box.

One morning I came across a HARO opportunity that sounded interesting. The request read:

> "Are you a female entrepreneur with a currently active business or nonprofit? Then we'd love to hear from you. We're looking to feature female entrepreneurs on [site name] via a series of email interviews. Once those are published, we'll do a massive list similar to [link to sample]."

The following thought immediately raced through my brain:

*"I'm not successful enough for this feature."*

Bam! It had happened. Without hesitation. In 1.3 seconds flat. That toxic story crept into my mind like a stealthy ninja ready to steal my opportunity—and my joy.

Read the request again. Is there anything—*anything*—in that request that says the entrepreneur has to be at a certain level in her business or earn a specific revenue or have received numerous awards?

No! It simply says that they were looking to "interview female entrepreneurs with a currently active business or nonprofit." Well, that was absolutely me for sure. So why on earth did my mind immediately go to *"I'm not a good fit because I'm not successful enough"*?

Because we are conditioned to avoid putting ourselves in situations that could cause us to be rejected by our peers and outcast by society. Aside from the basic necessities of food, water, and shelter, the next most important need we crave and depend upon in order to reach our full potential is connection with others. To be rejected and outcast is to be disconnected. To be disconnected is to live on the outskirts of society, where things get scary. Where the criminals live. Most of whom are there because of some sort of disconnection in their lives.

Joseph H. Baskin, MD, in an article titled "What Makes a Criminal?" (*Psychology Today*), shared, "A child who grows up with all basic necessities cared for will look different than one who worried about where his next meal would come from or whether trauma lingered outside the door . . . repeated insults of a similar nature can overwhelm even someone with high resiliency." All of this can lead to the development of criminal behaviors at worst, or a sense of avoidance at best. In either case, the resulting outcome is internalized similarly. Being rejected means you might become outcast from society, which can lead to becoming disconnected and therefore alone in this world. The question then becomes: Why take a chance and put yourself out there in the first place?

In my example, here's how my mind processed the situation: If I put myself out there (by submitting myself for consideration) and was rejected, obviously I'm not good enough to include. That equals disconnection. And all of this happened in a split second when I read that request—but why?

We learn about connection, and consequently disconnection, at an early age in school. Those past experiences create a foundation in our developing minds of what it means to belong, to be included, or, conversely, to be excluded. I remember it clearly happening to me in fourth grade, when I wore a beautiful black dress with a floral print on it to school for picture day, along with a lovely cream-colored bow in my long, dark hair. My mom had helped me pick out my dress and get ready for school that morning. I left the house feeling like a million bucks.

That afternoon, as I sat in class, a boy I had a crush on at the time sat behind me in one of my classes and tapped me on the shoulder to tell me I had a giant green booger in the tissue on my head. He then proceeded to snicker about his joke with a couple friends nearby.

First, I was in shock. Then, my face flamed with embarrassment. My feelings were shattered. And I immediately hated that boy.

How could I have gone from feeling like a million bucks that morning to never, ever wearing that beautiful bow again? Because of rejection. Because of fear of being disconnected.

It may seem inconsequential. A schoolgirl crush. A boy making jokes. But it was a pivotal experience in my childhood that has led to many toxic stories over the years about me being good enough to belong.

Perhaps you can relate. Maybe you had a similar experience as a child that greatly shaped the way you show up in this world due to fear of rejection or not fitting in. Feelings of not being good enough, smart enough, pretty enough, trendy enough—just *enough*—to fit in, be part of the group, be included in the activity, attract your crush, get the promotion, or lead your team.

As I've written this book, I've experienced new toxic stories myself. I've been pivoting, transitioning, and making a lot of changes in my business. Like, burn-it-all-down-and-start-again type of changes—which are all good and needed. However, while I'm usually quite adept with handling big doses of change, even I have my limits.

Day after day, week after week, as I've navigated these changes and launched new services and offers, I put myself out there for criticism and rejection—for disconnection. The more I did, the more fear rose up. The toxic stories and thoughts started rolling in like tidal waves crashing full force into the shore:

» *Maybe this wasn't such a good idea.*
» *Maybe I'm not cut out to offer this service.*
» *Maybe no one really needs what I have to share.*
» *I must have it all wrong, since no one is signing up.*
» *Maybe I'm not cut out to teach this content.*
» *Did I make a mistake by going down this path?*
» *Should I have not changed anything in my business?*
» *What if I just killed off my whole business—and I have to close the doors?*
» *I have no idea what I'm doing!*
» *I suck at business because I can't make this work.*
» *Why did I think I could do something like this?*
» *I should just go get a real job, where they'll pay me to show up every day.*
» *Why is everything so damn hard all the time?*
» *Why don't I have more of this whole business thing figured out?*
» *How is so-and-so doing this and I can't?*
» *I must not be good enough to do this.*
» *I hate running a business, it's such a drain.*

See how easy it is to go down this rabbit hole? Once a toxic story starts to take hold, it can take on a life of its own. The corresponding negative self-talk affirms the story and provides us with "evidence" to support our story. As we start to believe the story and negative self-talk, we could even begin to feel shame around the feelings that are coming up or our perceived incompetence. One thing leads to the next and, before we know it, we've spiraled out of control over something that is untrue and unfounded. We fail to take action for fear of rejection and disconnection—and then we feel ashamed. Here's what it might look like in action:

Your business is growing and you're considering hiring an employee. You know this is what you need in order to sustain the growth and reach your goals. You're excited, yet extremely nervous at the same time. You've never been in a leadership role and aren't sure you have what it takes. This is where the toxic story begins. You conduct interviews and find someone you think will be a great fit. You extend an offer, and a start date is set for two weeks in the future. The closer the employee's start date gets, however, the more nervous you feel. The toxic story continues to build momentum. *"What if I don't have what it takes to be a leader? I don't want to mess this up. And I don't want my business to suffer, either. Maybe I'm just not cut out for having employees."* As you spend time fretting and worrying over your inability to lead this person, you don't take the time to prepare yourself and your business for the new hire. You're not even sure you're going to follow through with it after all is said and done. As the day arrives for your employee to begin work, you realize you don't have anything ready for him and your schedule is packed that day. He walks in, eager to get started, and you're already frazzled, wishing you could hide under a rock. You tell him that he's going to spend the day shadowing you and secretly hope that he'll just quit, because you're "just not cut out for this." You think to yourself, *"See, I'm going to make a terrible boss. I wasn't even ready for my first employee today and it was such a waste of a day!"* The toxic story is gaining momentum because of the negative self-talk you've been feeding yourself, which has in turn impacted your actions, giving you plenty of examples (or "evidence") to substantiate the toxic story that you're not cut out to be a leader. In reality, you simply needed to create a plan for onboarding your new hire and then follow the plan.

Have you ever found yourself in a similar situation? Most of us have. Whenever we encounter a new situation, one in which we have no experience, we immediately begin to tell ourselves stories about our level of competency, even if we have nothing to base it on. We forget that we were once new at the things we excel at now and that we have to start somewhere in order to gain competency. But our rational mind has a tendency to take a back seat when our fight-or-flight center starts to kick in. We're wired to protect ourselves, so even if this situation isn't going to lead to imminent danger and death, it could possibly lead to rejection and disconnection, which is still a very dangerous situation.

We can slap a smile on each day, pretend as if all is well, and get to work. But inside, we might feel like we're slowly suffocating. The fears we concoct may not necessarily be real or come true, but they feel true to our cores. It seems as though someone is shouting at us to sit up and pay attention. To look at the evidence and consider the negative outcome. Because, maybe, just maybe, we really aren't cut out for this whole leadership thing after all.

Take a look at the list on page 51. Highlight or underline any of the phrases you've said or thought about yourself before. Then, use the space below to write about a time when you had a toxic story and the negative self-talk you experienced.

_____

_____

_____

_____

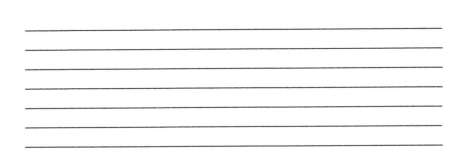

Read back over your toxic story and negative self-talk. Would you ever in a million years say any of these things to your best friend? (*I hope you said* no!) I wouldn't dream of saying any of the hurtful and mean-spirited things I said to myself to my best friend—and if I did, I fully expect we wouldn't be friends for much longer. You deserve better than this, and that's why I wrote this book: to help you overcome these toxic stories and negative self-talk, so that you could break free of the lies and uncover the truth and strength of who you are.

Now that you have a better understanding of what toxic stories are and you're not feeling so alone anymore, because everyone struggles with them, we're prepared to move forward. In the next section, we dive deep into where these toxic stories come from so we can better understand them in order to overcome them.

## Where Do Toxic Stories Come From?

As long as there have been humans on this planet, we have told ourselves stories about what we can and cannot do. What we can and cannot achieve. Who we can or cannot be. How good or bad we are compared to others. It's not just a leader condition, it's a human condition.

In the following pages, we explore the four different areas my research has uncovered that these toxic stories come from: nature, nurture, culture, and fear. Each area includes examples and Journal Prompts to allow you time to reflect on your own toxic stories and explore where they came from. This is important for the work we'll be doing together later in the book on clearing out these toxic stories from your life, so as much as you might want to avoid getting uncomfortable here, make sure not to skip this section.

We can see from the previous section that these toxic stories aren't doing us any good. But where do they come from, and why do we struggle with them? After working with hundreds of leaders throughout my career, and researching this topic, I've identified two main reasons we have these toxic stories.

First, our brains are trying to protect us from taking too big of a risk. Have you ever heard the term *lizard brain*? This is our innate human brain function that protects us from danger. It keeps us from stepping off the edge of that cliff and falling to our death. It uses fear as a guiding light to help us steer clear of danger. The funny thing is, sometimes fear is a bad fear (don't touch the campfire flame or you'll get burned) and sometimes fear is a a good fear (I'm going to take a chance and lead my team to do something incredible by breaking all the traditional rules this year). One causes you to recoil; the other has you leaning forward with bated breath in anticipation of what's to come. Admittedly, it can be downright hard to tell the difference. The next time you find yourself in a situation in which you're not sure whether the fear is a good fear or bad, pay attention to how your body is responding. You'll likely have shortened breath and an elevated heart rate with both, but are you truly recoiling from what lies ahead, or are you secretly excited about it and just afraid to fail?

The world around us has taught us to be afraid—to stay in line and do the "right" thing by following the rules or something is wrong with us. Following the rules of what is expected of us in our culture can make us feel connected to the greater whole of society, while at the same time leave us feeling isolated and alone (even though, oddly enough, most of us feel the exact same way). When we do dare to step outside of the lines that have been drawn for us, we're regarded with caution, we're labeled "weird" or "strange," our creativity and individuality are stifled, and, more often than not, we give in to the pressure and fall in line. When we fall in line, we start to lose our voice and our courage to try new things. We finish school, find a stable job, get married, have kids, work until we retire, and that's life. Anything outside of that is, at best, absurd. What about the woman who doesn't wish to get married? Or the couple who would rather live a life of travel and adventure versus finding a stable career and settling down to live in the same home for the next 40 years? Consider the couple who doesn't choose to have and raise a family—or the one who has 10 children. Are any of these choices bad or wrong? No, but they are out of alignment with what society teaches us is "normal" and "expected." The same is true in business and in leadership: We're led to believe that typical rules and expectations are the only true and right way. What if you led your team with loads of empathy, compassion, and a nurturing spirit, instead of a demanding, unsympathetic, "my way or the highway" mentality?

Now, I'm not here to tell you to buck the system or defy authority. Laws and rules are in place to help us live and work together as a society. I'm just saying we can all thrive in our own ways outside of what is taught to be the typical path or standard.

We have more opportunities now than ever to explore new ideas, opportunities, and callings. To try something new and different. The generations who came before us paved the way for us to do more. It's time to step up and into our power, our authority, our individuality to live and lead beyond our wildest imaginings. Because when we do so, we are able to create an even greater impact in this world and leave an enduring legacy for generations to come, demonstrating that each of us may choose our own unique path and not be outcast from society.

These cultural stories are beliefs we hold as a society. They've been formed over many years and passed down through generations. They hold us back from reaching our full potential, not only as individuals, but as a society in whole. It's time to toss out those old, disempowering stories and begin to weave powerful new ones that will support us in our individual journeys, as well as help us grow as a society.

In the coming pages, we explore the four main types of toxic stories people have. Throughout my years of research and working with leaders, nearly all stories fall into one of these four types.

Along with each type description is a prompt for you to explore and uncover any toxic stories you may be holding in that area. I urge you to take the time to consider what stories you might have in each area. Most of us have stories in each of the four types. The more time and effort you take to reflect on and answer each prompt, the more you progress you will make in your leadership journey. We have to first learn where we are on our journey, in order to know where we want and need to go.

## Nature

Many toxic stories we hold stem from our own personalities—the internal wiring we're born with, you could say.

We might be hardwired to be tough on ourselves and hold ourselves to extremely high standards or expectations, or we might be inclined to be more pessimistic or super critical of ourselves. We might be overly optimistic, thinking everything will work out and never exploring the pitfalls of any situation we find ourselves in. Or we might have a tendency to worry endlessly, always stressing out about every finite detail of every waking moment.

You may or may not be aware of your natural tendencies when it comes to the toxic stories you hold. I encourage you to explore those tendencies in the space provided. When you've jotted down a few ideas, go deeper. Then go deeper still. Continue exploring those tendencies and asking, "Are there more?"

These natural tendencies will come into play later in the book when we talk about identifying where new stories come from and overcoming those stories. So dig in deep!

*Journal Prompt: My natural tendencies (personality traits) are:*

*(Example: I have a natural tendency to play it safe. I don't enjoy stepping outside my comfort zone, so it's hard for me to try new things.)*

_____

_____

_____

_____

_____

_____

## Nurture

Other stories come from those who raised us or had influence in our lives when we were growing up. We saw our parents struggling to manage their schedules and time, and now we do, too. We heard our mom say something negative about herself, which has now become our own story (such as *"Ugh,*

*I'm terrible with numbers!"*). We learned these stories because our families pass them down through generations.

There are also stories we adopt from others outside our family (like friends, coworkers, and supervisors) who could be the cause of some of the toxic stories we hold because of the ones they hold personally.

Examples of stories about leadership might sound like:

> » "If you want something done right, you just have to do it yourself."
> » "You can't find good help anymore."
> » "Kids these days have no work ethic."

When we hear these stories on repeat, we start to believe they are true, whether they're about our circumstances, our teams, or ourselves—and whether or not they are true. After a while, you don't even question them anymore, as they become part of who you are.

Think about the ways that those around you have influenced your own personal stories.

*__Journal Prompt__: What stories have those around you imparted to you?*

*(Example: My dad always said, "If you want something done right, you have to do it yourself.")*

_____

_____

_____

_____

_____

_____

## Culture

In a similar vein as nurture, the culture in which you were raised plays a big role in the toxic stories you tell and believe about yourself.

Cultural expectations of what our lives and jobs should look like play out in the media every day. They play a big role in everything from our image to the way we talk, the kind of jobs that are considered desirable, and the ever-present "keeping up with the Joneses" mentality, which creates an overabundance of comparisonitis (how we measure ourselves against those around us).

These standards of success are constantly pushed down our throats through advertisements and posturing posts on social media. It's hard to escape the pressures of living up to these standards and always feeling less than perfect.

Regardless of the culture you grew up in, you've likely developed some beliefs about yourself, personally and professionally, as well as your place in society.

Journal about the culture you were born and/or raised in. We'll see later if these cultural expectations play a role in any of the toxic stories you find yourself experiencing.

*Journal Prompt: What cultural expectations or pressures were you born into or raised with?*

*(Example: My culture expects women to be seen and not heard.)*

_____

_____

_____

_____

_____

_____

# Fear

We all experience fear. If you're human, you have experienced fear at some point, whether it's an existential fear (purpose in life, fear of death, etc.) or a more everyday type of fear (public speaking, leading a team, etc.).

The more we open ourselves up to trying new things, the more fear shows up.

Did you know that there's actually a technical term for this? *Neophobia* is the fear or dislike of anything new or unfamiliar. And the more unfamiliar the territory, the more our minds try to protect us from it by crafting stories about why it's not a good idea. Cue new toxic stories!

If you find yourself constantly in new territory, you might be battling more toxic stories than usual. If your life or business tends to be fairly stable, these might not come up as often for you. It's also important to remember that we can experience seasons where there are heaping spoonfuls of change and trying new things, and others where things are more symbiotic.

I'd guess that one of the reasons you're reading this book right now is that you're facing some significant changes and challenges in your professional life. Maybe you've just taken on your first leadership role or perhaps you've been struggling for a while and are ready for some support.

In either case, for this next prompt, journal about the things that have been keeping you up at night recently.

*Journal Prompt: What is keeping you up at night right now? What new things or changes are you dealing with that leave you feeling uncertain and anxious?*

*(Example: I just hired my first employee and I'm worried I don't know what I'm doing.)*

***

Now that we've discussed the four main types of toxic stories we tell ourselves and we've taken the time to reflect on each type, as well as, journal about the personal stories we hold in each area, next we explore when and how toxic stories show up in our lives.

## Our Experiences Shape Our Stories

Regardless of the type, stories most often come from an experience we had during our lifetime. In this section, we explore how our experiences shape our stories and how these stories impact the results we achieve.

One concept I've used throughout my work with leaders over the years comes from the book *Change the Culture, Change the Game* by Roger Connors and Tom Smith. In the book, the authors introduce the Results Pyramid, in which three critical elements of organizational culture work together to produce results. The concept states that our experiences shape our beliefs, our beliefs influence our actions, and our actions produce our results (whether positive or negative).

I've applied this concept to the idea of toxic stories to better explain how our stories hold us back from reaching our full potential. My version states:

*Our experiences create our stories, our stories influence how we show up in the world, and the way we show up in the world determines the impact we will have.*

We can see this represented in two concepts, described below: the Toxic Story Cycle and the Healthy Story Growth Model.

The Toxic Story Cycle occurs when a person has an experience, which leads them to create a toxic story about their abilities. If the person gets swept away in this cycle, she then looks for supporting evidence of her toxic story, otherwise known as confirmation bias (as we discussed earlier in the chapter). When she finds evidence to support her toxic story as true, she then continues to experience similar situations where the story is proven true in her mind, thus perpetuating the cycle. As you see, once we're stuck in this cycle, it can be difficult to break free. We essentially become victims of our circumstances, which then control our outlook on the world around us and impact our ability to grow and thrive as a leader.

**Toxic Story Cycle**

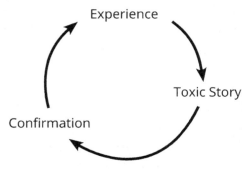

By contrast, as we see in the Healthy Story Growth Model, when we learn to question the stories we hold as truths and assess their accuracy, we can develop new, healthy stories and grow in our leadership roles. This model puts us in the driver's seat. We are in control of what we learn from our experiences and how we allow them to impact us moving forward.

**Healthy Story Growth Model**

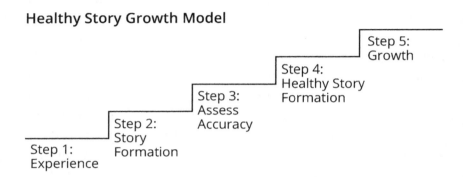

An important note about the Healthy Story Growth Model is that, although it represents upward movement and growth, there are times where we succeed (the risers) and times when we have plateaued or stagnated (the treads). Sometimes, we may even occasionally take a step or two back down the staircase. But in this model we are working toward being proactive, taking responsibility for our actions, and continuing to make progress in a healthy and positive direction. The Healthy Story Growth Model is very proactive, whereas the Toxic Story Cycle is reactive.

Even people who typically function within the Healthy Story Growth Model might find themselves stuck in a Toxic Story Cycle. The key to remember here is to pull yourself out of that Toxic Story Cycle as soon as you realize you're stuck in it so you can get back to being proactive and climbing the staircase of the Healthy Story Growth Model.

As noted in the previous section, our stories often come from an interaction we've had with our parents, bosses, coworkers, friends, or culture or society in general. We learn through our interactions and those experiences are what create our stories, whether healthy or toxic.

Our stories then influence the way we show up in the world. If we hold a healthy story, we show up fully for ourselves and are more likely to reach our goals. However, if we are holding onto a toxic story, we might shy away from opportunities that could help us reach our goals and create the kind of impact we dream of having in this world.

*Journal Prompt*: *Take a moment to think about how you show up in the world. What experiences shaped the stories you hold that have led to the way you show up?*

Here are a couple examples to help you with this prompt.

EXAMPLE 1

*Action*: You don't hand off all the day-to-day tasks to your team that you should, which keeps you from being as productive and effective in your role as leader and leaves you feeling overwhelmed and behind all the time.

*Belief*: If you want something done right, you should just do it yourself. You find it hard to trust your team members and let go because you don't have time to waste redoing their work.

(Side note: Your beliefs are the stories you're telling yourself. Some are true; others are clearly not true. It's not good or bad; it's simply what you believe because of the experiences you've had. We have to create new experiences in order to shape new beliefs, so that we can change our own actions.)

*Experience*: In high school, you were assigned to work on a project with another classmate, who was a complete slacker. In order to get a passing grade, which affected your ability to pass the class, you had to take on more of the project than you were assigned. You went to your parents for advice and your dad said, "We want you to get into a good college and there's no way that's going to happen if you don't pick up the slack on this project. Always remember: If you want something done right, you should just do it yourself!"

*How is this impacting your role as a leader?* You love and respect your dad. He's been a hard-working provider for your family your whole life. He's done the best he can with what he had.

Rather than exploring the message he shared with you throughout your career, your confirmation bias has kicked in and you've only noticed those moments when everything aligned with what you were taught. You've thought to yourself on many occasions, *"Dad was absolutely right. If you want something done right, you should just do it yourself!"* You've also not considered that there's another way to do things and that sometimes done is better than perfect.

The impact it's having on you now is that you're stressed out by leading your team and are still doing all the tasks yourself because no one else seems to do them correctly. Your business is struggling because of your inability to let go. Your team is frustrated because they know you don't trust them, and they're starting to question whether or not this is the right job for them. They're not inspired to do great work, because they know you're just going to nitpick it to death or turn around and re-do the whole damn thing—so why even bother? They can't keep going like this (and trust me, they won't!). It's time to make some serious changes.

*What new experience do you need to create for yourself to bust through this belief?* Start with something small and relinquish full control of it. Set yourself up for success by writing some notes to share with your chosen team member about what you expect out of this project: who is involved, what needs to get done, when it needs to be completed, and general guidance on how it needs to be done. Ask your team member to repeat back what you shared about the project so you can be certain that you didn't miss any steps (and so you know they were listening!). Set a follow-up meeting with your team member, and let them know to come to you with any problems they encounter that they can't handle on their own, but that you fully expect them to be able to handle this project from start to finish on their own. Finally, let go and trust that your team member will get the project accomplished within the time frame and parameters you've discussed with them.

EXAMPLE 2

*Action:* You have a hard time communicating effectively with your team. Why don't they just do what needs to be done without it always being a struggle?

*Belief:* My team members should listen the first time and get it right. There's no excuse why someone can't follow my orders exactly. If they don't, there will be consequences.

*Experience:* Your middle school soccer coach was pretty tough, and she expected her orders to be followed exactly—without having to repeat herself. Often, punishments were doled out to those who didn't get it right. You were not a fan of running extra laps after a long, grueling practice. Today, you feel like you can talk until you're blue in the face to your team and no one seems to listen. You might as well be talking to a brick wall.

*How is this impacting your role as a leader?* Your team is scared of you. They don't come to you with questions about projects or assignments, which means they're not doing them correctly the first time. It's causing a lot of extra work and frustration among the whole team. Everyone is exhausted, and morale is low.

*What new experience do you need to create for yourself to bust through this belief?* Try a new approach to your communication. If you've been primarily communicating verbally, try following up that conversation with some bullet points in an email. Or ask one of your team members to take meeting notes and send them out to everyone afterward. You can also ask your team how they receive information best. Not everyone processes information the same way. Some people are visual learners, whereas others learn and comprehend best by listening. Try communicating your message in multiple formats to meet everyone's needs up-front—and avoid confusion and mistakes later.

***

Now it's your turn. Take some time to work through your own experiences and how they are impacting you as a leader. I've provided space for you to explore four scenarios. You may wish to work through all four, or perhaps you may only do a couple. You might even get on a roll and decide to do more. The choice is yours. You can also come back to this exercise any time you feel like you're not fully showing up for yourself in some area and wish to explore why.

*Action:* _____

_____

*Belief:* _____

_____

_____

*Experience:* _____

_____

_____

_____
_____
_____
_____
_____

*How is this impacting your role as a leader?* _____

_____
_____
_____
_____
_____
_____
_____

*What new experience do you need to create for yourself to bust through this belief?* _____

_____
_____
_____
_____
_____

***

*Action:* _____

_____

*Belief:* _____

_____
_____

*Experience:* _____

_____

_____

_____

_____

_____

_____

_____

*How is this impacting your role as a leader?* _____

_____

_____

_____

_____

_____

_____

*What new experience do you need to create for yourself to bust through this belief?* _____

_____

_____

_____

_____

_____

***

*Action:* _____

_____

*Belief:* _____

_____

_____

*Experience:* _____

_____

_____

_____

_____

_____

_____

_____

*How is this impacting your role as a leader?* _____

_____

_____

_____

_____

_____

_____

*What new experience do you need to create for yourself to bust through this belief?* _____

_____

_____

_____

_____

***

*Action:* _____

_____

*Belief:* _____

_____

_____

*Experience:* _____

_____

_____

_____

_____

_____

_____

_____

*How is this impacting your role as a leader?* _____

_____

_____

_____

_____

_____

_____

_____

*What new experience do you need to create for yourself to bust through this belief?* _____

_____

_____

_____

_____

_____

## Stories Can Keep Us from Reaching Our Full Potential

When a child is first learning to walk, it's an exciting time. The adults around them cheer the child on, saying things like "Come on, little one! You can do it!!" They rush to grab their cameras to capture the precious moment, and then they share the photos and videos on social media for all their friends and family to see and share in the celebration.

When that same child falls, as naturally they will do when they first begin to toddle about, how do the adults respond? Do they berate the child? Tell the child how stupid they are? Walk away and tell the child to think about the way they failed?

Of course not! They pick the child back up, dust them off, and set them back on their feet to try again. They say things like "It's okay. You can do it! Try again!!" After many attempts, the little one gets the hang of it and starts zipping around. But it's certainly no easy feat. One study found that a child took an average of 2,368 steps and fell on average 17 times per hour when learning to walk (*Psychological Science,* October 2012). That means that not only does the child not have to give up, but the adults must persist with a positive mindset, as well.

At some point, we all learned to walk (physical limitations excepted). We took thousands of steps and fell dozens of times, but we persisted and eventually we learned to get around successfully. As a child, there was no doubt in our mind that we could, and would, learn to get the hang of this walking around thing that we saw all the adults doing.

But somewhere along the way, we started to believe that we might not be capable of learning how to do everything we wanted. Or doing everything we wanted. Or even being good enough to have everything we wanted.

Where does this come from, and why does it happen?

Somewhere along the way, we typically have an experience that changes the way we view ourselves and therefore changes our belief about our capabilities or, at the very least, makes us question our abilities.

My friend Bethany had an experience that changed her whole belief about a particular industry, as well as the actions she took within that industry. She came into a new space seeking new opportunities to expand her business and help a new type of ideal client. When she was new to the industry, she was excited about the possibilities that awaited her, so she reached out to make connections with people she admired who were farther along in business than she was. However, she was met with a considerable amount of condescension and cliquiness. One particularly scarring incident occurred when she reached out to someone she admired and that person, in turn, wrote an email to her list about the situation—about how she was tired of people trying to "pick her brain" and take advantage of her success. Obviously, this was mortifying for my friend. The person she had reached out to had to have known that she was on her email list and would certainly see the email. What a passive-aggressive way to get your point across (not to mention a bad example to set for those who are following you).

Bethany's story began to form from this experience: "No one wants to help you in this online creative space." With each passing week, the story rooted deeper and deeper. She faced other experiences similar to this one, heard fellow creatives saying the same things, and saw others unfolding online and in her inbox. She started to say things like "I feel like the 'we all support and help each other' stuff is just something people say. Yes, there's talk, but you don't see as much action. People say that, but then also say a lot of stuff that negates it. It's BS in most cases."

As we talked about this situation, Bethany said, "It's caused me so much pain. So much depression. So many setbacks." She wished she'd never even ventured into the creative space to begin with.

It's important to note here again that not all stories are toxic. Some are healthy. But even healthy stories can easily turn toxic, if we feed them. Bethany could have continued to look for stories, situations, and experiences that fed this monster and let it keep her from moving forward. But instead, she used the stories that were forming based on her experiences, and the experiences of those around her, to propel herself forward—and to make intentional choices *not* to succumb to the stories and stay stuck or, worse, quit. She distanced herself to understand whether she was the source of the problem, or if it was stemming from somewhere else. When she realized the source was external, she unfollowed toxic people online, set healthy boundaries for herself, and looked for new avenues in business to explore. Bethany told me that she has been "so much happier and more fulfilled" since realizing this and shifting her focus.

I love Bethany's ability to pull back and self-reflect. It's a strong character trait that served her well in this instance and will serve her well into the future, no matter what she chooses to do. Her story exemplifies what it means to take note of the experiences you're having, reflect on them, and then change course if they're not serving you.

In the coming pages, I share more examples of damaging stories that I, my clients, and my friends have found ourselves stuck in throughout the years. If you've been having a hard time coming up with your own stories, stick around. By the end of this book, you'll have a better idea of the ones you're holding onto that are holding you back from reaching your full potential as a courageous and confident leader.

# Chapter 2
# Discover the Role Stories Play in Our Journeys

*"The question isn't who's going to let me; it's who is going to stop me."*

*- Ayn Rand, Russian-American writer and philosopher*

Stories are important in our journeys. They teach us about life. They teach us about ourselves. They teach us about what we want and need. If we listen closely, the lessons we're learning can help craft a happier, more joyful life aligned with our values.

In today's age, instant gratification plays a big role in the stories we tell ourselves. When we try something new and we're not an instant pro, we immediately feel like a failure and start to form stories about our competency, intelligence, and self-worth.

Sometimes, this inner drive helps us reach harder for our goals in order to achieve them. Other times, it can become debilitating, leading us to think, *"I'll never make it!"* because we didn't experience great success on the first try. We can either let those stories define us and influence the next steps we take in a negative way, or—as my friend Bethany from Chapter 1 did—we can use them as fuel to make necessary changes in order to reach our bigger goals and dreams.

Rather than letting our experiences defeat us, we should use them to propel us forward. But remember: It's not the actions that we take that will lead to us achieving different results next time. It's the experiences we have and create for ourselves that will do this.

The next time you feel like a failure after trying something new, do this instead: Do something else that you're good at to remind yourself that you are smart, talented, and capable of doing hard things.

*Example: Feeling frustrated with teaching a new team member a task? Stop and work on a client project to stop the negative story in its tracks and boost your self-confidence.*

Once those endorphins are released into your brain, you'll be sitting on cloud nine, ready to tackle the world! When you return to the task you had been working on, I bet you'll get a different result this time. Why? Because you've changed your immediate experience. You've bolstered your confidence by experiencing something you're talented at, which will spill over into the work that you're doing elsewhere. If you find learning something new to be overwhelming and frustrating, try taking frequent breaks and intersperse the new activity with ones you're already competent at in order to keep the momentum and your spirits flying high.

Many times, our personal stories influence and can negatively impact the stories we tell and believe about ourselves in our professional lives. An off-hand comment during a pivotal time, a pattern of damaging behavior from someone we love over several weeks, months, or years, and choosing one option over the other because it was easier in the short term (but could have brought far greater satisfaction in life over the long term) can all influence the stories we tell ourselves down the road. These experiences can impact us for many years into the future, and working through these situations is typically not a quick fix.

Do you remember the old saying *Sticks and stones may break my bones, but words will never harm me*? A nice thought for the playground, but the reality is that the way people speak to one another often causes longer lasting bruises on our souls and in our minds than sticks and stones ever could. Words stick with us and shape us. Here are a few examples you might relate to:

» A verbally abusive parent, partner, or other relationship
» A teacher, coach, or guidance counselor's off-hand remark about your abilities
» A sexist, elitist, or racist supervisor or boss

The examples could go on and on, but I bet you already have a situation in mind that tells your own story.

If we believe the things being said about us by these toxic people, then we begin to craft the story that we're unworthy or incapable. As we discussed in Chapter 1, we may subconsciously start looking for other scenarios or situations to support this story, thus proving that we are, indeed, unworthy or incapable of doing something—which keeps us from imagining our own potential and thus keeps up from reaching it. This is what I refer to the "pile-on effect," when one story leads to another, and then another, and before long we have so much evidence supporting the initial story that was untrue, that we have no choice but to believe it to be true.

Although this is a less-than-ideal situation, not all stories are bad, and there's something we can learn from each of them, even those that are deep-seated in our minds and our hearts.

In this chapter, we explore the roles these experiences play in our lives, both past and present. We discuss how these stories aren't necessarily all bad and how they are designed to give us perspective, protect us, and help us grow.

## Stories Protect Us

One of the first, and most important, things to understand about the stories we tell ourselves is that they exist to protect us.

They protect us from making bad decisions and poor choices, or finding ourselves on the outskirts of society.

That last one might not seem that important. Who cares if you exist on the outskirts of society? Think again! When we encounter a situation that puts us at odds with our social group (whether family, friends, or society as a whole), we may start to concoct stories to protect ourselves from being cast out, which then impacts how we show up in the world.

In Abraham Maslow's Hierarchy of Needs pyramid (originally from a 1943 *Psychology Today* article titled "A Theory of Human Motivation"), we learn that all humans have basic needs that must be met (represented at the bottom of the pyramid) before we can ever reach out full potential—or, as Maslow described it, self-actualization, where creativity, acceptance, meaning, and potential meet.

Our basic or physiological needs, such as breathing, food, water, shelter, clothing and sleep, can be found at the base of Maslow's pyramid. Without these, we have no foundation upon which to build ourselves up.

The second and third tiers represent our needs for safety and security, love and belonging, and it is within these tiers where our toxic stories come into play. In these tiers, we often tell ourselves toxic stories to protect us from ridicule, being labeled as strange, weird, or different, and being outcast by our families, friends, and society as a whole.

## Abraham Maslow's Hierarchy of Needs

**Self-actualization:** Morality, creativity, spontaneity, acceptance, experience, purpose, meaning, and inner potential

**Self-esteem:** Confidence, achievement, respect of others, the need to be a unique individual

**Love and belonging:** Friendship, family, intimacy, sense of connection

**Safety and security:** Health, employment, property, family, and social stability

**Physiological needs:** Breathing, food, water, shelter, clothing, sleep

It's important to pause here and share a little-known fact about Maslow's theory. Cindy Blackstock, University of Alberta professor and member of the Gitksan First Nation, has said that many people are unaware that Maslow was stuck on the development of his theory. In 1938, he went to visit some friends in Canada who were researching the Blackfoot (an indigenious people of Canada) reserve. Karen Lincoln Michel wrote on her blog (A Digital Native American; April 2014), "'It was then,' Blackstock said, 'that Maslow learned of the Black-foot beliefs that shaped his model.'"

The Blackfoot nation's beliefs were focused on self-actualization as the base of their tipi model, where they believe tipis reach to the sky. The next tier is community actualization and finally community perpetuity. "Blackstock explained cultural perpetuity as something her Gitksan people call "the breath of life." It's an understanding that you will be forgotten, but you have a part in ensuring that your people's important teachings live on," according to Barbara Bray (on her site, Rethinking Learning, in March 2019).

## Blackfoot Nation's Beliefs

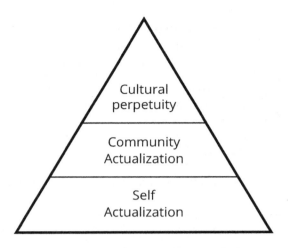

The Blackfoot's focus was on the community as a whole rather than the individual, whereas Maslow flipped their beliefs, focusing on the individual primarily and finalizing his motivational model that we know so well today.

Maslow's theory states that we need to experience connection and belonging among social groups, regardless of how large or small, before we can achieve belonging and self-esteem or ever truly reach our full potential (self-actualization). Without the sense of love and belonging, those greater aspects of our being are nearly impossible for us to reach, let alone achieve.

Consider something for a moment: Are you the same person at home as you are at a networking event? Your place of employment? With your girlfriends? At an amusement park? We all reserve parts of us for only the closest friends and family—parts the rest of the world doesn't see: the goofy parts, the nerdy parts, the parts others might view as different, at best, or perhaps even downright strange. These are reserved for those we feel most comfortable with, and hidden away from the larger society for fear of being an outcast.

It's kind of like going on a first date. Each person is on their best behavior. You sit up straight in your seat, keep your elbows off the dinner table, and take small bites of food. But once you get comfortable in a relationship, there's nothing holding you back. One day you look up and you're joyfully diving face-first into that giant doughnut, getting powdered sugar and cream filling all over your face without a care in the world (this may or may not be a true story!). You're experiencing unconditional love and belonging, which offers a sense of comfort and acceptance. In turn, you feel more confident and your self-esteem is boosted by the acceptance you've found.

With each progression up Maslow's hierarchy, we're closer to reaching our full potential as a human being.

Through the years, I've found that our leadership journeys follow a similar path to Maslow's Hierarchy of Needs. After learning about the Blackfoot model, what I've learned about leadership is much more in alignment with their beliefs. First we must focus on ourselves in order to fulfill a greater service to our community, and the world, as a whole. We must go through certain steps, and achieve specific milestones, in order to reach our full potential and impact as leaders. That is why I developed the Leadership Impact Model, which describes our journey from self-awareness as a leader to how we can achieve maximum impact in the world. Layer by layer, as we develop our leadership skills, we build the Leadership Impact Model from the ground up with the goal of creating maximum impact at the top.

At the base of the Leadership Impact Model is **self-awareness.** This is a successful leader's most essential skill, which is why it's at the base of the pyramid. Without self-awareness, we don't know what we're doing well or where we need improvement. Everything else is built from having a solid understanding of who we are and how we show up in the world. A lack of self-awareness can lead to denial and ineffective leadership, because we don't have a full grasp or understanding of how our words and actions impact those around us or what the realities of our personal strengths and weaknesses are.

**The Leadership Impact Model**

For example, a leader who refuses to believe that she could try a different form of communication with her team in order to improve overall team performance is in denial about the impact she can have on her team. Without the self-awareness to stop and ask, "What else could I be doing to ensure my directions are clear with my team?" she may never improve.

Without recognizing the role you play in your team's performance, you won't be able to continue moving up the pyramid to the next tier or have the opportunity to reach your full leadership impact potential.

The next tier is **personal responsibility.** Once we're aware of our strengths and where we need to improve, we must have complete and total acceptance and ownership that we are responsible for the outcomes in our own leadership journey. We are the source of our successes, as well as our challenges and frustrations. Without taking ownership and personal responsibility, we can never reach our full potential and impact as a leader, nor will we be able to model this critical behavior for our teams. At this level, we also realize the importance of admitting our mistakes and missteps and apologizing when we fall short. Vulnerability plays a big role here and helps us create better connections and rapport with our teams.

The middle tier is **capabilities.** In this tier, we fully know what we can and cannot (or should not) do. We understand that we need other, talented individuals around us to complement our strengths and fill in the gaps where we are weak or where our time isn't best spent. We realize we cannot do it all or do it all alone; other people in the world can do many things far better than we can. In this tier we learn how to trust our own capabilities and let go of those things that are not strengths or where we should be spending our time.

The next tier is **purpose.** At this point in our leadership journey we truly know why we are here on this earth and what we are meant to do. Nothing will stop us from fulfilling our purpose, and that begins to create clarity for us and a fire in our hearts. We start to cast off those things no longer serving us and to be more intentional about where our focus lies and what we're working on. People begin to follow us at this tier because they want to be part of something much bigger than themselves—and we clearly know the way. At this tier, we're building mutual trust, respect, and rapport with our teams.

Finally, the top tier is **impact.** Because we've worked on our self-awareness, taken personal responsibility for our success and growth, identified our capabilities and released the rest to our team of experts, and found our purpose, we can now reach our full potential and greatest impact. At this level, our energy and enthusiasm around our purpose are like flames drawing moths in the dark. People are excited by the clarity of our vision, motivated by the goals and milestones we've communicated, and ready to go on the journey alongside us. At this level, our teams are fully supportive of the mission and vision we have and would do anything for us. We're not just leading a business or even a team at this level, we're changing lives with the impact we're able to have.

Many people avoid the base tier of the Leadership Impact Model (self-awareness) altogether because it simply brings up too many hard truths to face. It's easier to believe that people like us than it is to know they think, for example, we're not a great communicator. However, we'll never truly get our team on board and reach our full potential if we don't learn how to be a more effective communicator. In order to develop those skills, we must first be aware of the weakness, take responsibility for the weakness, and work on developing that skill.

With both Maslow's Hierarchy of Needs and my own Leadership Impact Model, you can easily see how these toxic stories can pop up all the time. Our brains write these stories to help protect us and to keep us safe. However, these stories aren't doing us any favors.

These toxic stories hold us back in many ways. They make us feel timid and afraid, they may even have us acting in direct opposition with what we know is best for a particular situation or in alignment with our genuine self.

*Journal Prompt: Have you ever experienced a situation in which you tried to convince yourself to have a different opinion, thought, or feeling about what was going on or who you are be-*

*cause it was too hard to face the truth? As a reminder, additional reader resources can be accessed at www.ashleycox.co/stories.*

_____

_____

_____

_____

_____

## Stories Give Us Perspective

Stories help us look at situations from a different perspective, in both healthy and toxic ways.

When we tell ourselves positive stories, we can see the opportunities in and navigate various situations with a healthy balance. It becomes easier to pitch a new idea at work, reach out to that dream client you've always wanted to work with, or handle difficult conversations with your team when needed.

On the flip side, if we're busy telling ourselves toxic stories, we might only see the bad in a situation. Perhaps you tell yourself you're not good at math every time the quarterly reports are due. You dread those damn reports every quarter. You just know you're going to spend hours pouring over the numbers and probably make a mistake (or two). It's the worst. By the time report week rolls around, you've worked yourself up into a state of frustration, and you do indeed spend hours fretting and worrying over the reports before you ever sit down to actually do them. You've created a self-fulfilling prophesy of sorts: You expected the worst to happen and it did. Now have even more evidence that you're not good at math, the reports take you forever, and you probably made a couple of mistakes. It's a vicious cycle.

However, these toxic stories can also give us perspective and help us see our own worth and value. In the summer of 2018, I was nominated for and won a place among the Rising

Tide Society and Honeybook's "20 on the Rise" initiative. (According to the Rising Tide Society and Honeybook website, the initiative was created to "recognize individuals who are making an impact in the creative economy and freelance industry . . . [and to be a] celebration of individuals who are making waves and raising the tide, rocking their respective industries through hard work and creativity.")

When I learned of my nomination, I didn't share it with anyone, not even my best friend or my mom. I didn't share the fact that I had received a coveted spot on the list, even though I knew two weeks prior to the official announcement.

The day of the big announcement came and as I eagerly scanned the list for the names of my closest friends, I found a few, but not everyone I was expecting to see there. I had submitted heart-felt nominations for small business owners I believed in with my whole being, and they weren't on the list.

Suddenly, I had a sick, sinking feeling in the pit of my stomach. They weren't there, but I was. The toxic stories began to roll in like a dark and ominous storm:

» *Who am I to be on this list?*
» *There are so many other more deserving people than me!*
» *Why didn't so-and-so make it? They're far more talented than I am.*
» *I'm so unworthy of this recognition. My business isn't doing* that *great.*

I actually wrote replies like this one to people who sent me congratulatory messages on social media:

"I can't even imagine being the team who had to make these selections. It had to be so hard. I was completely blown away when they told me I had been chosen. And then felt an immediate sense of guilt and unworthiness because I knew if

I had been chosen, that meant someone else hadn't who was just as, if not more, deserving."

I'm sure I said thank you somewhere in those streams of DMs, but the overall message I was telling others was "Thanks, but I'm not good enough/I don't deserve this honor/I'm not as talented."

Not only was I beating myself up, but—even worse—I was brushing off their congratulatory messages as if they didn't even matter. I was essentially saying, "Thanks, but no thanks." Why couldn't I just say, "Thank you very much!" and leave it at that?

The longer I thought about it, the more I felt there was a lesson to be learned: I could be humble in this recognition, without putting myself down. I could appreciate the fact that my hard work had been recognized without letting it go to my head. Yes, there were other people just as, if not more, deserving than I, but everyone couldn't be chosen and that was okay.

As you can see, although I went down the rabbit hole of toxic stories at first, I quickly realized that this wasn't a healthy place to go. I learned the lessons I needed and gained some much-needed perspective. I was able to not only empathize with those who had not been chosen, but I used this opportunity to reflect on the fact that I, too, was worthy of being chosen. And last, but most certainly not least, I was reminded that my value comes from what I do each and every day for my clients and my community, even when no one is watching and praising my efforts, which is most important of all.

*Journal Prompt: Can you recall a time when you didn't think you were worthy of an award you won? A recognition you received? A promotion? Write about that time below. Dig deep about the thoughts and emotions that came up for you, using the following questions.*

*What was the situation?*

_____

_____

_____

_____

*What did you tell yourself about your inability to handle what was needed?*

_____

_____

_____

_____

_____

*How did you feel before, during, and after the situation?*

*Before the situation, I felt: _____*

_____

_____

*During the situation, I felt: _____*

_____

_____

*After the situation, I felt: _____*

_____

_____

*What can you learn from this that you can use positively the next time you're faced with a similar situation?*

_____
_____
_____
_____
_____
_____

## Stories Help Us Grow

The stories we tell ourselves have another interesting benefit (at least, for most of us): They can keep us humble.

A good, healthy mindset is important to showing up as the best version of ourselves as possible. But when things start to slip into the land of over-confidence, things can go sideways for us.

My friend Beth turned a toxic story into a great learning experience. As a true introvert, Beth enjoys running an online business and working from home. However, she started to explore her options to expand her business locally and was invited to speak at a live event.

Beth was both excited and nervous for this opportunity. She knew the woman hosting the event, which added a sense of comfort to stepping outside of her usual environment. Beth also learned that she would be one of three speakers and wouldn't have to kick things off, which, of course, took some more pressure off. But public speaking was still wildly outside of Beth's comfort zone and the audience was a group of people who weren't typically what she had defined as her "ideal client," so her nerves ran high.

On the day of the event, as she listened to the other pre-sentations, Beth got a sinking feeling that her presentation wasn't good enough. The keynote presenter was a woman who had been on the popular TV show *Shark Tank* and received $100,000 to fund her business venture.

As Beth listened to the woman's inspiring business journey, her own toxic stories began to play:

> » *Who am I to be here speaking to these people?*
> » *What could I possibly share that they don't already know?*
> » *Was this a massive mistake?*
> » *My presentation won't be good enough!*
> » *There are men in this room and my presentation is titled "Content Her Way." (*Her *way, as in for women! Beth didn't know this would be a mixed crowd.)*

But there she was, slated to speak, and she wasn't about to back down.

Of course, her nerves were strong at the beginning of the presentation but eased as she got into the flow. Sometimes, that's all it takes: to just get started. Somewhere in the middle, Beth recalled, she felt a palpable engagement in the room—from women and men alike.

At the end of the workshop, Beth was approached by some of the men in the group who commented about how great her presentation and the content was that she shared. They joked about how it was called "Content *Her* Way," but how it certainly applied to everyone in the room, regardless of gender.

So imagine, just for a minute, if Beth had allowed those toxic stories to get the best of her. Imagine if she had feigned an illness and not followed through with her speaking engagement.

She would have missed out on:

> » Opportunities that are changing the very face of her business,
> » Exploring a new client base she hadn't considered before,

» Honing and refining her skills and realizing she had the power to reach more people than she ever imagined before, and

» Further developing her skill set—which will take her and her business to the next level.

When we allow our toxic stories to become our truths, we miss out on so much potential for opportunities and growth.

The next time you feel the pull of fear, not being enough, or unworthiness, remember that what your heart desires most is often found on the other side of those toxic stories.

If we hold onto healthy, positive stories about who we are, what we're capable of, and how we wish to show up in the world, they can keep us moving forward with great momentum.

Healthy stories can also mean that we tell ourselves we don't know everything and we're willing to learn from those around us—and we should always be on a mission to grow and evolve.

Although those may sound like toxic stories, they're actually not! They are healthy because they keep us humble and working to improve ourselves on each step of our journeys.

What's toxic is telling ourselves stories about how we're never going to be able to learn, do, or be something. Those are the kinds of stories that hold us back and keep us small. They don't promote a healthy mindset. In fact, they do the opposite: They keep us thinking and living from a place of insecurity, fear, and doubt.

When we can break through what is not true and instead focus on our opportunities to learn and evolve, we'll be working from a place of humility and growth instead.

# Chapter 3

# **Identify Our Stories**

*"I learned to always take on things I'd never done before. Growth and comfort do not coexist."*

*- Ginni Rometty, CEO, IBM*

One of the most difficult parts of navigating our own stories is trying to determine which are healthy and which are toxic.

We can most easily see toxic stories playing out in other people's lives, especially close friends and family members. However, when it comes to identifying them within ourselves, it can be a bit more challenging. Oftentimes, we're too close to the story and can't see it for what it is.

Remember the story in Chapter 1 about what the host of *Someone Knows Something* said? "It's easier to believe the story we want, rather than the truth we're in."

We don't necessarily *want* to hang on to some of these toxic stories, but they simply become what we know and we get stuck in the Toxic Story Cycle we discussed in Chapter 1. We've had other toxic stories for so long that we don't even realize what they are or that they are harming us in one way or another.

A client of mine, Angel, was struggling with delegating. She knew she needed help in order to continue growing her business, but she kept avoiding it at all costs. When I asked her straight out why she was avoiding hiring help, she said, "It's going to take me too much time to train someone. I can just do it faster myself. By the time I explain what I need done, show the person how to do it, teach them the system, etc. I could have already been done."

Feeling like there was more to her story, I asked her, "What if training wasn't an issue?" In other words, what if the person she hired had all the skills she needed? To that she replied, "Well, hiring is expensive. If I don't have to pay for help, then I can do something else to grow my business, like hiring a marketing firm."

I followed up: "And how are you going to manage more work than you already have on your plate right now?"

She just stared at me, obviously considering this question for the first time.

Before she could respond, I asked, "Angel, what are you really afraid of?" And this is where things started to get good.

Angel was fearful of being in charge of someone else. She had only ever been an employee, an individual contributor, someone responsible for her own work. She wasn't sure she has what it takes to be a leader and she didn't want to mess up. She had worked for terrible bosses in the past who had made her life miserable. She didn't want to be that person to someone else.

The reasons she gave for why she was avoiding hiring help were just surface stories to which everyone would nod along with understanding and empathy—stories that she didn't have to explain and stories that didn't force her to face these deeper fears, when were truly what were holding her back.

This is not uncommon. I hear similar stories all the time with the same surface-level stories.

When you're busy formatting blog posts, talking to tech support, and designing graphics for your social media pages, you're not building relationships with potential business partners, nurturing relationships with clients, or taking action on the innovative ideas that will grow your business to the next level.

A one-time investment of time to train a team member can yield a long-term return of time into your daily schedule. The money you pay an employee is less than the worth of your time, which should be spent on high-level tasks that only you can do. And you will be an incredible boss, because you care and because you're taking the time to invest in yourself through education (like this book!), training, and mentors.

What you might be trading, for a little time and money, is a lot of time and money.

In this chapter, we discuss how to identify your toxic stories and work through some exercises to help you uncover even the deep-seated ones you've been holding onto for years—those you may not even realize you have, which are keeping you from reaching your full potential and becoming the courageous and confident leader you want and need to be.

## Look Out to Look Within

The first and most effective way I've discovered to identify our own toxic stories is to look without first, in order to look within. What do I mean by this?

The world is filled with people living with their own toxic stories. You just have to pay attention to see which ones each person holds as their own personal truth!

We hear the stories in our day-to-day interactions. Here are a couple examples:

» You stop to grab a latte at your favorite local coffeehouse. As you chat with the barista, you ask, "How's your day so far?" She responds, "I'm here . . . " (released with a long, sad sigh).

- What's her story? Why is she so despondent? Is this a dead-end job for her? Or maybe she's dealing with some tough things at home. You don't know. What you learn from this interaction is to pay attention to how you're showing up in the world. When asked about your day, how are you responding? This can tell you a lot about what stories you're carrying around with you. Perhaps you hate the job you're in and you reply with a lackluster "Another day, another dollar."

» When you arrive at work, you encounter a co-worker who quickly walks by you and whispers out of the corner of his mouth, "Watch out for the boss today. He's on the rampage!"

- What's going on with your boss? Is he upset because sales are down and he just got chewed out by his boss? Did he have a fight with his wife before he left the house? Did he just receive a terminal illness diagnosis? Again, we don't know what's going on with him, but his outward-facing behaviors tell a deeper story. If sales are down and he got chewed out by his boss, he might be feeling like he's a failure or incompetent. If he got into a fight with his wife, he might be feeling like nothing he does makes a difference or that she doesn't appreciate how hard he works. If he just found out he has a terminal illness, he might be thinking about how life can be so unfair and why people are worried about such silly little things at work today.

*Journal Prompt*: *Think about the past 48 hours and answer the following questions. As a reminder, additional reader resources can be accessed at www.ashleycox.co/stories.*

*How did you show up in the world?*

_____
_____
_____
_____
_____

*Why did you show up this way?*

_____
_____
_____
_____
_____

*How do you think people perceived you when you showed up this way?*

_____
_____
_____
_____
_____

*Is there a toxic story that contributed to the way you showed up that you need to explore? If yes, journal about it here.*

_____
_____

_____

_____

_____

Over the coming days, pay close attention to how those around you interact with and respond to the way you are showing up in the world. Then, consider how the way you are showing up is impacting you on a daily basis. Keep a journal of your observations and findings to uncover patterns and explore the toxic stories you are living with.

Now that we've taken a look around us to start identifying surface stories within ourselves, let's discuss more deep-seated stories we developed when we were very young that we've been holding onto for a long time. Those are a bit more challenging to unearth and explore, because they are such an ingrained part of us.

## Discover Deep-Seated Stories

Next, it's time to consider the deep-seated stories we may be holding onto. These are the stories that have taken up residence in our minds and have been hanging around for years (maybe even decades). Often, these stories stem from something we experienced as children. Even though it's hard to see or understand this at first, once we dig a little deeper into the stories we're telling ourselves, we can usually trace them back to a pivotal time in our childhood. To best explain this, let me share a personal story about how my own deep-seated stories showed up during a business trip and how I worked through them before they caused any major problems.

I work as a subject matter expert (SME) for the Society for Human Resource Management (SHRM). A couple of times each year, I'm asked to travel to Washington, DC, to participate in workshops during which I help develop content for the organization and the HR profession. Although I had been on these trips multiple times before, one particular trip was different.

As I settled into my seat and the facilitator began to give instructions for the workshop, my toxic story reared its ugly head. I was sitting in a room surrounded by 40 of my HR peers from around the world when, all of a sudden, a wave of "I'm not good enough" thoughts began to wash over me. I felt them in every fiber of my being.

- » *Why are* you *here?*
- » *You don't even practice "real HR" anymore.*
- » *You're not nearly as smart as the other SMEs.*
- » *What if you screw this up? How stupid will you feel then?*
- » *You're not sophisticated enough to be here. These people are from big cities all around the world, and you're from a small town in a rural area.*
- » *Maybe you should just pretend to get sick and leave now.*

And on, and on, and on.

I broke out in a cold sweat as these thoughts raced through my mind. They rolled through my head like a freight train I couldn't stop.

*What am I doing here? What value could I possibly add this workshop—or this organization?* I slowly started to find myself agreeing with this negative self-talk around my toxic story.

After what felt like an eternity (which was very possibly only a whopping total of two to three minutes), I finally realized what was happening.

The negative self-talk was simply the manifestation of a toxic story I was telling myself. I took a deep breath and started to push back against the stories, asking myself, **"Is this**

**true?**" I then began to transform the toxic story and negative self-talk into a healthy and more factual representation. The chart on the following page outlines the transforming process.

As I worked on transforming my toxic stories, I paused to look around the room and consider that others might be experiencing some of the same self-doubts. I decided to send positive energy and encouragement out to the other people in the room, figuring we could all use a bit of good energy.

The voices in our heads that tell us we're not good enough are what author Brené Brown calls "gremlins," in her book *Daring Greatly,* in which she further explains, ". . . those manipulative monsters . . . derive pleasure from destruction." And it's so true. In that moment, those toxic thoughts were trying to destroy my self-worth and sense of belonging in that room.

However, when I realized what was happening, I was able to recognize that those stories were false and transform them into a more accurate reflection of who I am as a person and what I brought to the table that day. I was able to refocus myself and go on to do the work I was entrusted with, alongside my peers. I was more confident, more relaxed, and able to focus on doing my best work, rather than worrying about not being good enough to have a seat at that particular table.

Where did this train of thoughts come from? Why did I feel like I shouldn't be in the room that day or at the table working with the other SMEs in the room? This was a question I explored later, after the workshop. As I reflected on my childhood, I thought about what situations or experiences might have led me to feeling not good enough to be included. I was never really an outcast in school, but I definitely wasn't popular, nor was I part of the "in crowd." I spent years trying to find a way to fit in, to belong, only for it to be clearly expressed that it wasn't going to happen. It started way back in elementary

| Toxic Story | Transformed Story |
| --- | --- |
| "Why are *you* here?" | "Why not me?" |
| "You don't even practice 'real HR' anymore." | "I practice real HR with real small businesses every single day." |
| "You're not nearly as smart as these other SME." | "I'm just as smart as the other SMEs. I can both learn and share valuable information." |
| "What if you screw this up? How stupid will you feel then?" | "We all make mistakes and we all have questions. That's why we're not doing this alone. That's why there are facilitators here to help us through the process. I have no reason to feel stupid. I'll be doing my best alongside 40 other people doing their best." |
| "You're not sophisticated enough to be here. These people are from big cities all around the world, and you're from a small town in a rural area." | "I belong here just as much as every other person in this room. Would I say this to anyone else in this room?" |
| "Maybe you should just pretend to get sick and leave now." | "I feel great and I'm excited to be here and contribute to the HR profession! Why would I leave and not get to be part of this amazing opportunity?" |

school with the comment about the bow in my hair. Perhaps it started even before then. But all along the way, I learned that I didn't fit. So when I showed up in this workshop, I immediately started to experience those similar feelings of not being good enough to be part of the "in crowd"—that I simply didn't belong.

Perhaps you've had a similar experience. Maybe there was a time when you were made to feel as if you didn't belong. When we carry those experiences with us, they create the beliefs and stories we hold about ourselves. And those stories hold us back from reaching our full potential—as human beings and as leaders.

Bronnie Ware, a palliative nurse from Australia, has worked with patients in their last three to 12 weeks of life for several years. Many of her patients would confess their biggest regrets and lessons learned during their final time on this earth. Moved by their stories and urging to not repeat the mistakes they made, she wrote the best-selling book *The Top 5 Regrets of the Dying.* In her book, she shares their most common regret of all: "I wish I'd had the courage to live a life true to myself, not the life others expected of me." Another common regret she shared in her book was "I wish that I had let myself be happier."

I can only imagine these regrets stem from worrying too much about what others think about us and trying to fit in with the crowd. The experiences we have in this world have us forming stories that hold us back not just for a day, a year, or a season; they can hold us back for a lifetime. What a powerful lesson to have to learn the hard way. What an unfortunate regret to have when there's no way to go back and do things differently.

Take these lessons from the dying and use them to inspire a change within you. Unearth those deep-seated stories, release the negative self-talk and the actions that stem from them, and become the person and the leader you want and need to be.

You don't know the kind of impact you can have when you show up fully as yourself in this world. At the end of my workshop, the facilitator told me the work I did was so good that their team "didn't make one change" to the work I had done. She also told me, "[I] wish we could find more SMEs just like you!"

To say I was humbled and blown away by her words is an understatement. Once I had shrugged off the feelings of being unworthy, I was able to show up, work with my fellow SMEs, and do my very best work. But I didn't need her validation at that point. I felt worthy and enough because I belonged at that workshop and alongside my peers.

As you can see, these toxic stories can come up for us over and over again. They can creep in when we least expect them, even when we know they're untrue. But, with a few tools to help us along the way, we can recognize when thoughts start to go off the rails and untrue toxic stories start to creep in that don't help us show up fully in this world. It's time to clear out your old stories and make room for some healthier new ones.

As we've discussed, the toxic stories we hold are often rooted in experiences we had when we were small children: an offhand comment during a formative time in your life or a parent's strongly held beliefs and views that they formed over their own lifetime. Perhaps it's where you grew up or the living conditions in which you were raised that have you feeling less than, or maybe you made a mistake in a public way and have carried feelings of shame around for years. Whatever the story, it's important to uncover it so you can move past it. We should not allow the experiences we had as children define us as adults and as leaders, nor hold us back from reaching our full potential. This journaling prompt walks you through the process of uncovering and breaking through your own deep-seated toxic stories.

*Journal Prompt: Think about a toxic story you've been telling yourself for years. (Examples: I'm no good at math. I could never be brave enough to ask for that raise. Who am I to lead a team?) Write it and then work backward. Where did this story come from? Try to pinpoint a time when you were a small child when you formed this belief. Perhaps you got a low grade on your first math test and someone told you that you were no good at math. Or maybe a parent fought a similar battle with asking for the raise they deserved and you overheard a conversation about it when you were growing up. Note: You may identify more than one story here and can repeat this prompt with each one. As a reminder, additional reader resources can be accessed at www.ashleycox.co/stories.*

To help you get started, here's a quick example:

*What is a long-held, deep-seated toxic story you've been telling yourself?*

I'm not as smart as the other people in this room.

*Where did this story come from?*

I went to a small, rural school that only offered a basic education. I didn't go to a school with unlimited funding and resources, so obviously I missed out on opportunities that others had.

*Who was involved in the forming of this story?*

Other people in the world who talked about their private school educations, the special magnet schools they went to, and the assistance they received from their school counselors, as well as college preparatory classes.

*What was their role in the forming of this story?*

They simply shared their experiences, and I immediately

felt I didn't belong, wasn't good enough, and didn't have the necessary education to be successful.

*Is this story about you true?*

Yes.

*Does this define your worth in this world or your capabilities?*

No. This story may be true, but it doesn't mean that I'm any less worthy or capable than the person sitting next to me. I used the resources available to me, studied and worked hard, and am every bit as capable and talented as someone who has had more opportunities and a better education.

*What is a long-held, deep-seated toxic story you've been telling yourself?*

_____
_____
_____
_____
_____

*Where did this story come from? (Go way back into your child-hood).*

_____
_____
_____
_____
_____

*Who was involved in the forming of this story?*

_____
_____
_____
_____
_____

*What was their role in the forming of this story?*

_____

_____

_____

_____

_____

*Is this story about you true?*

_____

_____

_____

_____

_____

*Does this story about you define your worth in this world or your capabilities?*

_____

_____

_____

_____

_____

Now, take five to 10 minutes and write your younger self a letter. Let her know this story isn't true. Tell her you are more than capable at doing whatever it is (math, being brave, leading a team, etc.) than you've been telling yourself. Tell the person who was involved in the forming of this story that their insecurities, fears, and doubts are their own, not yours.

Here's an example from the previous journaling prompt.

Dear Younger Self,

You may not feel so right now, but you are a smart, talented, and capable girl who will grow into a smart, talented, and capable woman. Every day, you show up with an excitement for learning and doing your best. You jump at every chance to get involved and try something new, and that is so important. It's something that will serve you well when you're all grown up. Don't worry about the kids from the other schools who have sophisticated after-school programs or other opportunities you might not have where you live. The way you show up in this world and how you use the tools and resources available to you will set you apart from the rest of your peers and help lead to your success. You are enough, you are worthy, and you have something to offer the world that is so special. Keep your head high and keep pressing forward.

Love,

Your Future Self


*Okay, it's your turn now. Write whatever comes to mind. Talk about how strong and brave and capable you are. Tell the younger version of yourself something you wish had been told to you. Talk about the strengths you had as a child and how those play out for you as an adult.*

*Get messy. Write freely. And don't stop until you have it all out.*

*Dear Younger _____(your name),*

_____

_____

_____

_____

_____

_____

_____

_____

_____

_____

_____

_____

_____

_____

_____

_____

_____

_____

_____

_____

_____

_____

_____

_____

_____

_____

_____

_____

_____

_____

_____

_____

_____

_____

_____

_____

_____

_____

_____

_____

_____

## Seek Feedback to Test Assumptions and Gain Insight

You've heard the saying _Feedback is a gift,_ right?

Sometimes feedback doesn't feel like much of a gift, especially depending on how it's shared with us, as well as the state of mind we're in when it's received. However, feedback is an invaluable tool in to help us grow both personally and professionally.

This section explores how to seek and use feedback to help us test our assumptions about the toxic stories we've been uncovering, as well as gain additional insights into other stories we may not know we're holding onto. When gathered and used properly, feedback helps us identify our patterns and story themes, as well as gain clarity around how we show up in the world. We may believe one thing about ourselves to be true, but getting feedback from those around us helps us see the bigger picture and can help us identify obstacles holding us back from reaching our full potential.

Before we discuss who to ask for feedback regarding our toxic stories, let's first talk about how to properly give and receive feedback, so we choose the right people to ask for feedback, as well as prepare to receive it fully.

## Giving and Receiving Feedback

If you've ever been on the receiving end of poorly given feedback, you know it can feel awful. And if you've ever been the person who's given feedback, you know it can be difficult to share your honest opinions without hurting the recipient's feelings. I've outlined five easy steps to help you have productive and supportive feedback conversations.

### Step 1: Choose Wisely Who You Ask for Feedback

This is not the time to ask just anyone for feedback. Identifying and discussing toxic stories can be a sensitive topic and may bring up a lot of emotions for you. Take care in who you choose to ask for feedback. Here are a few questions to ask yourself when making your selections:

> » Do I respect and value this person's opinion?
> » Does this person have my best interests at heart?
> » Will this person share openly and freely with me?
> » Will this person share in a way that will respect my feelings?

### Step 2: Set the Stage and Create Boundaries

It's important to set up the conversation properly. You don't want to call someone on the phone while they're in the middle of preparing dinner, with children running around, to ask for their feedback. They'll be flustered, distracted, and unable to support you in the way you need. Here are some tips to help you set up the conversation properly:

» Invite the individual out for coffee/tea in a distraction-free environment or to a virtual online chat.
» Let the person know that you value their opinion and would like to get their feedback on something very important to you.
» Ask for specific feedback regarding an area you would like more insight into. "I'd like to hear your feedback on me" is a recipe for disaster—both for you and them. Instead, say, "I'd appreciate your feedback on the way I communicated the recent change in our time off policy" or "I value your opinion and would like to hear your feedback around what I might be doing that's holding me back in the world" or something similar. This gives the person who is sharing feedback with you a clear and narrow focus and helps you prepare to hear the feedback better, rather than both of you being left to navigate unknown waters.
» Make sure to explain that this is a sensitive topic and you would appreciate tact in their response to make sure you're able to fully receive the feedback, but that you do want their full, honest opinion.

## Step 3: Prepare Yourself Mentally to Receive

This is a big step, so don't skim over it. In order to receive feedback and truly hear what you need to hear, we need to prepare mentally and emotionally to hear the feedback.

People often brush this off, citing that they are "great at receiving feedback." What they find, once they're in the middle of getting feedback, is that it's great to hear the good things about ourselves and extremely difficult to hear the not-so-good things.

We all love to hear what we're doing well, where we excel, and why people appreciate us. It boosts our confidence and morale, and makes us feel good that we've had a positive impact in the world (whether at home, in the workplace, or in your local community).

However, when it comes to hearing the hard stuff, we have a tendency to go into defense mode and start explaining why we acted in a certain manner, or we may simply brush off the feedback about a particular situation because we were "having a bad (or off) day."

When we act in this way, we're telling those sharing their feedback with us that we don't want to hear what they have to say, unless it's good. We don't value their honesty. When we do this, we turn off the feedback valve, and I can guarantee you that person won't be so willing to share their open and honest feedback with us again in the future.

When we don't hear the hard things, we refuse to look in the mirror and see ourselves from a different perspective—to acknowledge that we (yes, all of us) have areas to improve upon, to learn and grow from, and in which we can become a better version of ourselves.

Here are three ways to prepare yourself mentally and emotionally to hear and receive positive or constructive feedback. Remember that the feedback being shared with you:

1. *Was sought out by you.* You asked for the feedback, so you can't get upset by it. Yes, the feedback you receive may be difficult to hear or believe about yourself, but that doesn't mean you should get upset with the person sharing it.

2. *Will help you grow.* It's important to remember the reason you asked for the feedback: to help you grow! You won't be able to gain any lessons from the feedback if you're not ready to open up, consider a different perspective, and listen to the feedback.
3. *Is being offered by someone who cares.* This is why it's so important to choose wisely who you ask for feedback. You should respect this person and they should be someone who cares for you. It helps to remember that the person truly cares for you when they're sharing things that are hard to hear.

## Step 4: Listen without Judgment

This step ties in directly with Step 3. Part of preparing to hear and receive feedback is to remember to listen without making judgments, either about the person sharing the feedback or about how you receive and process the feedback.

What exactly does this mean, and how does it look in practice?

It means allowing the giver to share their honest feedback without jumping in to explain, defend, or talk our way out of anything we might be having a hard time hearing.

It means asking for the feedback and then listening more than talking, asking questions to better understand, and receiving the feedback in the same spirit in which we asked it to be shared. The feedback giver should be doing 90% of the talking.

When we immediately start judging the feedback we're receiving, we aren't allowing it to fully sink in, and we won't get the maximum benefit from it that we need.

We have to hear hard things sometimes in order to learn and grow. We have to be willing to view ourselves from someone else's perspective. When we do so, we get a clearer vision of how we're showing up in this world. Sometimes it's good. Other times, it's not exactly what we had hoped to hear.

Now, whether or not the feedback shared with us is accurate is a whole different situation. Remember: We're all viewing one another through the lenses of on our unique experiences and perspectives. The feedback we receive from one person may very well be the opposite of what we receive from another.

At the end of the day, we want to gather feedback from a few different people, from various areas of our lives, and assess the data we've received. Are there common patterns, themes, or perceptions? If so, then we may need to consider that feedback to be an area to work on.

## Step 5: Thank the Sharer for Their Feedback

This last step seems like the easiest—until we receive some really tough feedback. Even if the person who has agreed to share their thoughts unloads a bunch of feedback that we really don't want to hear, we always need to thank them for the feedback.

"Thank you for sharing your thoughts with me today" or "I appreciate you taking the time to share your feedback with me." It's that simple.

Again, we're not judging. We're simply thanking the person for being open, honest, and vulnerable. Yes, vulnerable. Sharing tough feedback with someone takes courage. Especially when you don't know how they're going to react. So make sure to thank the person to show gratitude, nurture the relationship, and open the door for future conversations.

\*\*\*

Next, let's discuss who you should reach out to for feedback.

## Feedback Sources

You can ask four primary groups of people for feedback: family, friends, coaches or mentors, and team members. Each group has pros and cons. We will explore these groups and discuss why you might wish to ask each for feedback and what to expect if you do.

### *Family*

Likely, our family members are the people who know us best. They've seen (and still love!) us at our best and our worst. They are typically the ones who will quickly call us out on our BS —but also defend our honor when we've been attacked or wronged.

However, this group can be the toughest all to ask for feedback. Involving family in this process can leave us wide open to responses that might leave us feeling deflated and could even lead to awkward times around the dinner table at the holidays.

The best way I've found to navigate this particular group is to be very selective about who you ask for feedback. Try to choose someone who will ask thoughtful questions, provide real, honest feedback, and (most importantly) honor our emotional well-being by framing their comments tactfully. We should also make sure to ask someone whose opinion we value highly.

If a family member doesn't meet these criteria, then move along to the next person on the list quickly. Otherwise, be prepared for just about anything!

### *Friends*

Friends are another great source for gathering feedback to help us uncover any toxic stories we have. Our friends also know us on a very intimate level, but differently than family members.

Friends have likely been with us through good times and bad. They've been by our side to celebrate successes, vent frustrations, and give advice when we have no idea what to do next.

Friends want to see us succeed, but they're also a lot less afraid to give it to us straight. They don't want us showing up and acting like a fool. They want what is best for us and they're often willing to be the "bad guy" by telling us what we truly need to hear.

Again, I caution: Choose the friend(s) to ask for feedback wisely. Ask yourself whether the person or people you're seeking feedback from will be open and honest with you and whether you truly value their insight and opinions, or if they don't really have much impact in how you show up in the world.

## Coaches or Mentors

One of the best places to get real, open, and honest feedback is from a coach or mentor. Whether we're working with someone specifically or have an unofficial advisor in our lives, their goal is to help us grow. And they know they can't help us grow by holding back, so they usually share feedback with us more freely on an ongoing basis.

If you've been in one of these relationships for a while now, you're probably very familiar with getting feedback from them, whether solicited or not. If you haven't, then seek out someone to be your trusted advisor. Getting referrals for a coach or mentor is the best way to make sure you're connecting with someone qualified and vetted. This person can be your secret weapon and help you push past roadblocks and challenges faster than anyone else.

I love working with my clients in this capacity. I often tell them that I'm their mirror. When they come to me with a problem or concern, I flip that mirror around to help them see the role they've played in whatever is going on. Sometimes it's positive; other times, not so much.

A mentor can help us gain a different perspective that is incredibly valuable and will help us navigate our own shortcomings in a way that feels good—so we can move past those shortcomings more quickly and reach our goals.

## *Team Members*

One of the most valuable ways to grow as a leader is asking our team for feedback. However, I know this might feel a bit . . . unnerving. (That's why I've listed this group last.) We truly need to practice receiving feedback and flex those feedback muscles before we dive into asking employees or team members for their input.

Asking employees for their feedback is one of the most difficult things we can do as leaders, as well as the most impactful. But remember: Our experiences create our stories. This goes for your team, too. If we react in a poor manner when they share their feedback, they won't be willing to share any in the future.

If you've had a hard time hearing tough feedback in the past, I urge you to start with any of the three previous groups of people we've discussed first: family, friends, and coaches or mentors. Get used to hearing hard things before asking your team for their feedback.

Once we feel ready to tackle the feedback conversation with our teams, here are some tips to navigate it with confidence:

> » Let the team know we want their feedback because we value their opinions and input, and that feedback isn't a one-way street on the team (i.e., you to them).

» Ask them to not hold back. We want to hear the good, the bad, and the ugly.

» Reassure them that whatever they share will not negatively impact them or their job—and mean it.

> *Side note: A great way to demolish trust with a team is to ask for their feedback, then lash out when they share something we don't want to hear.*

» Follow the steps in the "Giving and Receiving Feedback" section of this chapter to make sure we set ourselves—and our team—up for feedback sharing success.

The feedback from our teams will be some of the most insightful, helpful, and impactful feedback we'll ever receive when it comes to becoming the leader we want to be. Don't shy away from this incredibly valuable experience.

Something to be aware of in this situation is that all feedback does not need to be acted upon. However, if we never act on any of the feedback we receive, then the people we ask for feedback will eventually stop sharing it. That's exactly the opposite of what we want. Carefully consider what feedback to take action upon and what to set on the shelf. Feel free to follow up with those individuals who shared their input and let them know that you're taking action on their suggestions. This will build trust, rapport, and respect with those individuals and encourage them to continue sharing their feedback in the future.

While this section is fresh in your mind, write down one person from each category who you can reach out to for feedback:

1. Family _____

2. Friends _____

3.  Coaches or Mentors _____
4.  Team Members _____

\*\*\*

We've been through a lot of tough inner work in this chapter—from looking without to looking within and understanding how we're showing up in the world, to discovering deep-seated stories that are holding us back from reaching our full potential, to learning how to seek feedback from those around us in order to test our assumptions and gain insight.

As the quote at the beginning of the chapter said, "Growth and comfort do not coexist." The more uncomfortable we become, the more growth we will experience. I challenge you to continue getting uncomfortable in order to keep moving forward in your leadership journey.

Now that we have a better understanding of our toxic stories, next we discuss how to navigate those stories so they don't hold us back from becoming the confident and courageous leader we want and need to be.

# *Chapter 4*
# Navigate Our Stories

*"Make the most of yourself by fanning the tiny, inner sparks of possibility into flames of achievement."*

*- Golda Meir, Fourth Prime Minister of Israel
and First Woman to Hold that Title*

Once we become aware of our toxic stories, we can learn to navigate and manage them so they don't become the reason we're not reaching our full potential. We will also learn how to recognize them as they creep into our minds over the coming days, weeks, and months. Unfortunately, just because we're now aware of them, this doesn't mean they disappear altogether. However, when we can more easily see and understand what is happening, we can stop believing and living life in service to the toxic stories and, instead, focus on our goals and dreams.

In this chapter, we discuss how to recognize and navigate the stories we've been holding onto for a long time as well as those we will inevitably create and tell ourselves.

We do a lot more of the soul work during these next few sections, diving deep into our stories, as well as learning which situations, events, and people trigger new stories.

The exercises in this chapter are important because only when we become aware of the situation, can we create a plan of action for how to navigate (and eventually overcome) what is holding us back. This story about my client Sarah that highlights this beautifully.

Sarah came to me feeling frustrated and at her wit's end with her team. She told me she could talk until she was blue in the face but they just didn't listen to a word she said. They rarely did what she asked, lacked motivation, and were continuously late or called out of work. It was a pretty dire situation.

Sarah was certain she was doing everything she could to be a great leader and was convinced that she had simply hired the worst people possible. During our first call, she asked me if she could just fire them all and start over. Although she said this with a chuckle and told me she was just joking, I knew the feelings behind her question were deep and raw—and that likely Sarah had considered this approach seriously on more than one occasion. Sarah was desperate for a solution and felt she had exhausted all of the resources available to her.

After taking a deep breath and getting focused, we started to discuss the details about how she was leading her team. Through some self-reflection exercises we worked through together, Sarah soon came to realize that it was her own lack of leadership skills causing most of the headaches she was experiencing with her team (or, at the very least, certainly weren't helping any). She soon came to realize that her team wasn't the worst group of people ever to work together in one company together and that she had been playing a big role in the dysfunction of the team.

Once we uncovered the truth in her story, we began to work on specific leadership skill development that addressed Sarah's biggest problem areas. Her team quickly started turning around. Once she shed the toxic stories Sarah was telling herself about her team being the worst, she was able to make massive progressive and build momentum.

Now she's happier and more excited to lead her amazing team than ever before, and she avoided having to fire everyone and start over—saving time, money, and a lot of really hard conversations and headaches.

It's easy to get lost in the stories we tell ourselves:

> » "My team is the worst! I must have hired all the wrong people."
> » "If I only had A-players on my team, my business would run so much better."
> » "If you want something done right, you just have to do it yourself."
> » "You can't find good help these days."
> » "Kids are lazy and always on their phones."

Once we get so far down the rabbit hole, it's hard for us to see any other stories or options, thus limiting ourselves, our teams, and our businesses.

It's essential to look at our situation objectively and ask: "Is this true, or is this an old story I'm telling myself that's no longer serving me?" This is also where getting feedback is so valuable, as we discussed in Chapter 3. We must be willing to reflect on our own personal strengths and weaknesses, as well as the role we're playing in any given situation, to ensure were taking the right steps and getting the right help. Otherwise, we may be left spinning our wheels in frustration and never getting where we want to go.

As we discussed earlier, sometimes it's easier to believe the toxic story that we're in, rather than the truth of the situation. It becomes easier to fuel that story by looking for information that supports it (confirmation bias), rather than uncover the truth of the situation we're in and work on taking different actions to achieve a new and better outcome.

Let's take a deeper look at the toxic leadership stories we may be telling ourselves. We examine some of the most common stories, why and how these can be damaging, and ways we can navigate these stories to step into the truth of our situation.

## Common Toxic Stories

First, let's look at some common toxic stories we tell ourselves as leaders. These are all examples of stories I've heard from leaders and clients throughout the years:

> » "I'm not sure I'm cut out to be a leader."
> » "I should just hire someone else to manage my team."
> » "I'm not good at dealing with conflict."
> » "I have a hard time teaching others how to do what I do."
> » "If I want [insert any task here] done right, I should just do it myself."
> » "I have trouble letting go and trusting someone else."
> » "My team needs a lot of hand-holding or nothing gets done."
> » "I struggle with feeling confident enough to lead my lead."

Ever thought or said anything similar?

If so, keep reading to learn more about why these stories can be damaging to us and our business—and how to overcome them.

### More Toxic Stories

We hear all the time in business that having a positive and optimistic mindset is a key factor for being successful and winning at life and business. The same is true for our teams.

When we feed them stories that aren't true, are negative, or are damaging to their mindset, we won't get the very best effort from them, let alone have a cohesive, happy, and productive team.

Here are some of the toxic stories we tell ourselves and others about our teams:

» "I have the worst team. I hired all the wrong people."
» "My team never follows through. They don't do anything I ask them to."
» "My team doesn't care. They're not as motivated as I need them to be."
» "I wish I could just clone myself. Then I'd have the perfect team." (Important note: No, you will definitely not have the perfect team if you simply clone yourself. You need people with complementary skill sets, different perspectives, and diverse backgrounds to create a truly innovative, creative, and successful team.)

Damaging stories leaders have actually said to their team members include:

» "You never do what I ask. It's like you don't even care."
» "I obviously care more than anyone else on this team."
» "No one can do this right, so I'll just do it myself."
» "Just do the job you were hired to do—nothing more."

> » This is typically in response to a team member trying to bring a new idea, thought, or suggestion to the table. Often, the leader feels threatened when they say something along these lines.
>
> The absolute worst thing we can do is talk about one team member's performance, abilities, character, and so on to another person on our team. This will end badly every single time.
>
> If we need someone to vent we should find an individual we can trust and rely upon outside of our business—a fellow leader, coach, advisor, or mentor; anyone other than a team member—to discuss our frustrations and concerns with.

## Why Stories Can Be Toxic

The more we tell ourselves these types of toxic stories, the more we believe them. And the more we believe them, the more we find other bits of information to support them as being "facts."

As we discussed in Chapter 1, this is called *confirmation bias,* which simply means we look for information that supports something we already believe. This can become damaging because when we tell ourselves these types of stories, we have a tendency to make mountains out of molehills. The more we believe these toxic stories, the more our actions reflect those beliefs, which stunts our potential for personal and professional growth.

Take this scenario for example:

A new team member misses a minor task in a big project. When you learn of it, you immediately get frustrated and think, *"If I had just done this myself this wouldn't have happened. Ugh! I knew hiring help wasn't going to be worth it."*

By responding in this manner, we're using the information (in this case, the situation with the team member missing a minor task in a big project) to confirm previously held beliefs that "hiring isn't worth it" and "if you want something done right, you have to do it yourself."

But let's get brutally honest for a minute: Have you ever made a mistake? Missed a step in a project? Had something fall through the cracks on your watch? We're all human. We all make mistakes. We all miss things. And sometimes, especially when we're new to a job or a project, we just don't know what we don't know, which can lead to mistakes and missteps.

Blowing a simple mistake into a big ordeal to support your toxic story doesn't do us, our team, or our business any good. In fact, looking for ways to support those stories can do you quite a bit of harm.

Toxic stories and confirmation bias keep us from reaching our goals and chasing down our dreams. They can put a halt on the momentum we've created in our businesses and our lives and leave us stuck.

## Why We Tell Ourselves Stories

If we know they're not helpful, then why do we tell ourselves these stories? Why do we keep perpetuating beliefs that aren't serving us and are keeping us stuck? Because we're scared and unsure and just trying to figure things out as we go. As we discussed in Chapter 2, we concoct these stories to keep us safe—to protect us from being outcast or ridiculed by society, because in order to reach out full potential, we must belong.

It's overwhelming to learn something new in the midst of all the other things we have going on and the responsibilities we have. Everything we do in our businesses is a risk and opens us up for failure. And that's no small thing to bat an eyelash at, right? (I'm right there with you. It can be downright terrifying some days!)

Hiring and/or leading a team is something many of us can avoid or put off longer than we can other situations we find ourselves having to navigate as small business owners or people moving up the corporate career. But it doesn't have to be this way. We can learn skills and methods to navigate toxic stories so that they don't become a roadblock to our success.

## Navigating Toxic Stories

If we don't actively navigate our toxic stories, they can overcome us. But how do we do it? Whenever we realize we're telling ourselves a story about our ability (or inability) to lead, we must do our P.A.R.T. to navigate these stories in the moment:

1. **P**ause. Now that we're aware these toxic stories exist, we'll notice them more often. We all have them! When you notice one creeping in, pause and take a deep breath.

2. **A**sk. We need to ask ourselves: *Why do I believe this? Is it true? If not, what are some ways I can turn this negative story into a healthy one?*

3. **R**eflect. Take a few minutes to think about where this story came from. Was it something we heard at home when growing up? Or maybe one of our first bosses or mentors used to say something similar. Figure out where these thoughts and feelings are coming from so we can break down the toxic story.

4. **T**ake action. What can we do in the moment to take a different action that will lead to a different, and better, result? Do one thing that will move you forward.

This can be hard to think about conceptually, so here's a great example of someone who has created healthy stories in his mind and weeded out the toxic ones:

Michael Phelps is the most decorated Olympian of all time. However, he didn't just wake up one day in 2000 and say, "Hmm, the Olympics are taking place in Sydney this year. I think I'll try out for the Olympic team and win a bunch of gold medals."

He has dedicated his life to his career, spending hours upon hours practicing and honing his talent, and cultivating the mindset of a champion through the stories he's told himself every day and before every competition.

Michael has an entire visualization routine he goes through each time he competes. Every single detail is visualized—from the moment he steps up to the starting platform and the race begins to each stroke he'll take and where the walls of the pool are in relation to where he is in the water. He visualizes the turns he'll need to maneuver and even the final moment when he emerges from the water victorious.

He goes a step further to visualize potential pitfalls that may come up, like if his goggles fill with water or his swim cap comes off, so he can be prepared in any situation. But he focuses on winning and how he's going to win, not on toxic stories and negative self-talk that could hold him back from reaching his goal. And he certainly doesn't sit around in the locker room before an Olympic event thinking, *"I'll never win this race. My competitors are younger, faster, and better at the butterfly stroke than I am."* He knows he has practiced for this competition, that he brings experience to the pool, and that negative self-talk does nothing but set us up to fail.

In the same way that swimming is an athletic endeavor one must learn and practice daily to become skilled, so is leadership. As you know by now, I don't buy into the idea that leaders are born. Sure, it may be true for some, but not for the majority. Even those who were born with natural leadership qualities know the importance of continuing to learn, grow, and hone their skill set. If you think you're not cut out to be a leader, think again. It might just be a new skill to learn and practice.

In this section, we explore the negative impacts toxic stories can have on our self-esteem, our self-worth, our relationships, and our businesses and professional lives. We work through navigating old stories that aren't serving us and uncover which are, in fact, holding us back from reaching our full potential. And finally, we learn how to identify situations that trigger new stories so we can limit or avoid them altogether.

## The Negative Impacts of Toxic Stories

Holding onto toxic stories and engaging in negative self-talk not only keep us from reaching our full potential, but they have been linked to higher levels of stress, lower self-esteem, high blood pressure, and even depression.

The next few sections explore some of the implications of staying stuck in this unproductive cycle of toxic stories in various aspects of our lives.

### Self-Esteem

As I mentioned in the chapter opening, our self-esteem can take a big hit when we engage in and get stuck believing the toxic stories we hold on to. Merriam-Webster defines *self-esteem* as "a confidence and satisfaction in oneself; self-respect."

A friend of mine posted on Facebook about this very situation. She wrote: "I was never one to express myself and I've decided that it's no longer acceptable. I always preferred to blend in; preferring not to stand out. It felt safer that way. You see high school kids dying their hair, dressing uniquely and just wanting to express their individuality. That was never me. The idea of putting myself out there like that was like putting a giant target on myself to be rejected. This might be insignificant to a lot of people, but dying my hair feels like the first step to not be so afraid to stand out. So look out world!!"

I loved this post so much, because she had made the decision to no longer allow her toxic story of rejection keep her from living her life and doing what makes her happy. This simple scenario of changing one's hair color has deep emotional roots: fear of standing out and being rejected.

*Journal Prompt: Have you experienced a similar situation? What have you avoided doing because it made you stand out and fear rejection? What thoughts went through your head? How has this impacted your life? Take a minute to jot down some notes here. As a reminder, additional reader resources can be accessed at www.ashleycox.co/stories.*

_____

_____

_____

_____

_____

_____

_____

_____

_____

_____

Perhaps you made a comment like "I'm such a klutz!" or maybe you thought, *I swear, I can't do anything right.*

In either case, you immediately formed a story that wasn't necessarily the worst thing in the world, but certainly didn't build up your self-worth.

Once we begin our days with a toxic thought, it's a slippery slope to falling all the way down the hole and getting stuck in the vacuum of these thoughts for the rest of the day.

Next thing you know, you can't find your keys ("I'm so disorganized!"), you get stuck in traffic on the way to work ("Why can't I ever just leave on time so I can avoid all this traffic?"), you run into someone at the office and knock their papers out of their hands ("There's the klutz again!"), and on and on and on.

All day long, you're beating yourself up for little things, random situations, and accidents. You're tying a string of unrelated incidents together to support the story that you're klutzy, disorganized, and always running behind.

At the end of the day, you're feeling pretty crummy about yourself and wondering why you even got out of bed at all. You grab a pizza and a pint of ice cream on the way home—and then beat yourself up for making bad choices for dinner. You go to bed hoping and praying that tomorrow will be better—if you can just make it out the door without doing something stupid.

Do you see how quickly some burned toast or spilled milk spiralled out of control?

We must guard our thoughts carefully. Once we allow ourselves to believe one small, seemingly insignificant thought, it can quickly snowball into a bad day, week, or lifetime. And before long, our self-esteem is shot and we feel unworthy of anything good that comes our way. When we feel unworthy, we don't allow those good things into our lives, and our negative energy then pushes them away from us.

## Relationships

Have you ever heard the saying *You attract what you are?*

The Law of Attraction states that "like attracts like." People who have a low frequency—those who are insecure or self-deprecating—have a tendency to attract similar people into their lives. Those who have a high frequency—those who love and respect themselves—will attract those who do the same.

This is important to understand when it comes to our relationships. And not just the romantic kind, but all different types of relationships.

Whether it's a relationship with your spouse, friends, co-workers, or employees, we attract people into our lives who reflect the same frequency, self-worth, or value we perceive in ourselves.

We've probably both had that friend who is single and trying to find love. They've been on what feels like a million dates with every loser in town. Why is it so hard? Why can't this person find love? There has to be at least one decent other person in town, right?

Over the years, this person has lost their confidence. They start to craft the story that they'll never find love and they're destined to be lonely for the rest of their life. The negativity of this story surrounds them like a dark cloud, repelling the good.

Only when they see the worth and value in themselves will others be able to see it as well.

The old saying *We must first love ourselves before another can love us* is true (*maybe with the exception of our parents*). If you don't value and love yourself, you make it hard for others to do the same.

People with a healthy self-esteem don't want to be dragged down into a pit of despair. They're looking for someone on an equal playing field.

Next, let's take a look at this from a professional standpoint.

## Professional Life

Just as our personal relationships are impacted, our professional lives (whether you work for a company or own a business) are equally affected by the stories we weave for ourselves.

This is especially true when it comes to hiring employees.

When a business owner comes to me with the problem of not being able to attract or keep high-performing, top-level employees, we almost always find underlying reasons why that have to do with the business owner or leader.

I'm not going to sugarcoat this: If we're having a hard time attracting top employees, we need to look in the mirror and see what's being reflected.

No one wants to work for a leader who's always negative, has low self-esteem, and is constantly complaining about everything little thing.

When a leader is putting off low-frequency vibes, employees and potential employees can easily pick up on them.

We can't change our past. We can't change the experiences we have had.

What we can do, however, is use those experiences for good, rather than bad. To create new experiences for ourselves in order to form new, healthier stories.

Let's dive a little deeper into four of the common toxic stories that tend to crop up for leaders to understand where they may be coming from a bit better. I encourage you to ask yourself if you've ever said something similar and, if you have, to consider what impact it has had on your leadership journey.

### Toxic Story #1: I'm not sure I'm cut out to be a leader.

The people who have said this to me usually have a great deal of fear or anxiety about stepping into a leadership role. Here are a few examples of what we've uncovered for these individuals on their leadership journeys and why they feel they're not "cut out for this."

*A bad experience with a past leader.* Sometimes it's the last boss they had in their 9–5 job and sometimes it goes all the way back to a particular coach or teacher during their school days. They're worried about creating an experience for their team members similar to the one they had. They've sworn that they will never be like that person—which means they avoid being in a leadership role altogether. But that's the exact opposite thing to do in order to fix the problem. To fix it, you learn and do better.

*A positive experience with a past leader.* This seems kind of strange and the complete opposite of what we just discussed. A weird thing happens when we encounter greatness. The toxic stories form more quickly and more savagely. People who've worked for an incredible leader have a tendency to think they'll never live up to that person's level of excellence—that they'll never be good enough. So, why bother trying if they can't achieve the same greatness? You can see this happening in many other areas, too. Girls who had exceptional mothers want to grow up to be like them, but feel like they fall short as grown women and mothers themselves. Boys who want to grow up big and strong like their fathers often feel inadequate and defeated when they can't meet the standard they've established for themselves.

*Lacking a leadership example altogether.* Some of the clients I've worked with over the years have never worked a traditional 9–5 job with a boss. They went straight from school to working for themselves. For them, the transition from being a solo business owner to having a team is a precarious and terrifying one. Even though they're smart and talented, they've never seen leadership modeled outside of a school setting and have no idea how the dynamics of a team work in a business environment. They immediately start forming this toxic story because they really don't know what it takes to be a leader and begin to wonder if they can even do the job. Other toxic stories also start to form at this time, such as "Maybe this is as far as I was meant to go in business."

For those who have hired teams and still don't feel quite cut out to lead, they might find themselves saying something like our next toxic story.

### Toxic Story #2: I should just hire someone else to manage my team.

This one may not sound like a toxic story on the surface, but what I've come to learn in my research and work with clients is that this statement is often said to disguise self-doubt, fear, and insecurity.

Sometimes, it's said out of frustration. Other times, it's said because the individual really doesn't want to be a leader of people. You know what? That's okay. Not everyone wants to, or should, be a leader.

Some business owners want to keep their operations small, and hire a consultant or contractor every now and them to support their business. However, if we're looking to grow or scale our businesses with a team, we will be the leader. We will always be the leader no matter how many managers we hire to handle the team. We will be the leader for those managers. Saying we'll "just hire someone else to manage" our teams is another form of a toxic story in disguise. We're immediately admitting defeat if there's not a well-thought-out and strategic plan behind why we're hiring a manager. Now, don't get me wrong: There are plenty of great reasons to hire managers, and our businesses may one day need multiple managers. However, CEOs of big companies didn't just wake up one day and decide to hire a bunch of managers to escape being leaders. They hired them so that they *could* be a leader—a visionary.

Before we decide to hire a manager, ask the following question: "Am I running and hiding? Or am I making a strategic business decision?" What are our real reasons for hiring someone to lead and manage our team? Keep asking *why* to dig deeper and uncover the answer. If our reasoning is rooted in a real business case, then proceed. If we find ourselves running away from being a leader, then it may be time to do some inner work to clear out any toxic stories that are taking up space in our minds.

### Toxic Story #3: I'm not good at dealing with conflict.

Here's where my Southern side starts to reel: "If I had a dime for every time someone said this to me, I'd be a millionaire!" Growing a business and having a team are going to lead to conflict. I promise. Any time more than one person is working together, we're going to have conflict. (See what I did there?)

Conflict comes in many different forms. Depending on our sensitivity to conflict, we may experience this story more strongly than someone else—or maybe not as much. Think about it this way: Many, many times we've been scared about doing something in our businesses, but did it anyway. From starting the business and learning about business structures and taxes, to reaching out to those big influencers or national brands to talk about partnership opportunities, to figuring out what the heck a sales funnel is, to figuring out the perfect service or product offering for your client base. Without doing those things, we wouldn't be where we are today. We learned how to navigate those scary waters and find our way to dry land.

It's the same situation when dealing with conflict, upset employees, and poor performers. Facing these scenarios seems scary at first, but necessary to learn in order to grow to the next level in your businesses. Just like everything else we've learned along the way on our business journeys, this skill can be honed through learning strategies for developing techniques for handling conflict, as well as good ol' experience and practice.

## Toxic Story #4: I have a hard time teaching others how to do what I do.

I hear this one all the time. This one tends to be part fear and part excuse-making. It can easily become a story we're telling ourselves so we don't have to hire help and step into our leadership role.

We don't have to be an amazing teacher to show others how to do what we do and how we do it. We just need to have some systems and processes in place in order to get started. By writing down the steps we take, we can easily hand off tasks to new team members, who can then help you refine the training process for the next new hire.

I could offer endless examples of toxic stories that leaders often struggle with, but I hope these examples have given you some ideas for how to test and question the stories you are currently telling yourself.

We don't have to be perfect to lead well. As a matter of fact, some of the best, most successful leaders in history have openly admitted their weaknesses and sought support from others to help them grow. Doing so is a huge strength for a leader. Gone are the days when leaders are expected to never, ever show a weakness, a vulnerability, or a shortcoming. The days of being open, real, vulnerable and, well, *human* are here to stay. The greatest leaders have the self-awareness to know that their vulnerability is a massive strength. They know the value they bring to the table and continuously look for ways to keep improving.

# Navigate Old Stories

We can learn so much from the stories we tell ourselves, so it's best not to just ignore them and keep pushing forward. This is an opportunity to learn more about ourselves and do the deep inner work to continue improving.

That's why we begin with navigating old stories first. When we name the stories we've been telling ourselves for years, we take away their power. If we have old stories we've been hanging onto for a while, it's time to rid ourselves of those in order to begin the process of creating healthier stories to replace them and propel us toward reaching our fullest potential.

*Journal Prompt: Think about all the stories you currently have about yourself—the ones about your personality, how you show up in the world, the work you do, the type of spouse, parent or friend you are, and so forth. Take some time to explore all the stories you hold about yourself. You can always use more paper to fully flush out these stories.*

*What old stories are you holding onto? (Consider any and all stories, whether you think they're positive or toxic. We'll dive further into that in a few questions.)*

_____

_____

_____

_____

_____

*Where did these stories come from? (Refer to Chapter 3.)*

_____

_____

_____

_____

_____

*Who in your life held a similar story?*

_____

_____

_____

_____

_____

*Are these old stories true? This is the time to dig deep, look at the story objectively, and determine whether this is actually true about yourself.*

_____

_____

_____

_____

_____

*If not, why are you still holding onto them?*

_____

_____

_____

_____

_____

Here's a quick exercise to use any time a toxic story starts to come up called "60 Seconds to Suffer." I learned about this concept on Instagram Stories from Civilized Caveman (a wellness company specializing in gluten-free, grain-free, and paleo living and recipes), and it goes like this:

When you feel the toxic stories and negative self-talk creeping in, stop and recognize what's happening. Then, set a timer for 60 seconds and let that story play out to the fullest extent within that 60 seconds. Go ahead and think, *"I'm not good enough, I suck, I can't believe I made that stupid mistake,"* or whatever is coming up for you. When time's up, change your environment to pull yourself out of the toxic cycle. Take a walk around the block, run to your favorite coffee shop to grab a chai latte and work for an hour or two, or play a quick game of fetch with your pup in the backyard. By changing your environment and activity, you force your brain to shift gears and work differently, which allows it to put aside the toxic story and focus on something else. It's okay to have those thoughts—they happen to all of us—but it's not okay to stay there, or they'll destroy your forward momentum.

## New Story Triggers

Having a handle on old stories and where they came from can give us valuable insight into what triggers, or causes us to form, new stories.

In this section, we explore those times when we immediately formed a new toxic story about our leadership journey.

Through exploring our triggers, we can better identify when those sneaky toxic stories are creeping up and put a stop to them before they carry us away into the land of self-doubt and insecurity.

This section pushes you to look at yourself and your situations more objectively. This can be hard, so imagine I'm sitting there with you, warm cup of coffee in hand, and chatting about what's holding you back and keeping you stuck.

One concept we haven't explored yet, but that's important for this conversation, is that of *toxic positivity.* This is when we get tied down into thinking we must only have "positive thoughts" and "good vibes only" all the time.

If you're human, which I'm assuming you are since you're reading this book, then this is an impossible feat. Humans feel. We are emotional beings. To deny that we have both positive, high-vibe emotions, as well as negative, low-vibe emotions does ourselves a disservice.

It's okay to feel afraid, insecure, worried, and sad. These are all natural emotions and ones that all humans experience (well, except for sociopaths, but that's a whole different conversation). The challenge comes when we get stuck in negative emotions and allow them to dictate how we live our lives. It's important to acknowledge and experience the less-than-desirable emotions that arise in our lives, to treat ourselves with self-compassion and understanding, and then to learn how to release those feelings when they are no longer serving us. However, the more we fight against these feelings of unworthiness, fear, and doubt, the harder they are to move past.

I first learned the concept of toxic positivity from Shine Text, through their daily text messaging service, which had this to say about fighting the negative emotions: "Research shows that chasing happiness makes us more likely to dwell on and fight the non-happy feelings, but that can lead to more stress in the long run. It's not a fun cycle. Today, swap 'good vibes only' for 'it's OK to feel.' If an emotion comes up, greet it with compassion and try acceptance."

With everyone sharing their lives constantly on social media, it's easy to fall into the trap of thinking that everyone else in the world has their shit together. It's a good practice to remember, when you're feeling down, that most people only share their best days and weeks with the world—and keep all of the bad to themselves. If you find yourself having a hard day, week, or even month, try using this mantra from Kristin Neff, PhD, associate professor of human development and culture at the University of Texas and pioneer of research on self-compassion, quoted in *Psychology Today* (2012): "This is a moment of suffering. Suffering is part of life. May I be kind to myself in this moment. May I give myself the compassion that I need."

*Journal Prompt: It's time to explore what triggers you into forming new toxic stories. Think about the last time toxic thoughts crept into your mindspace and answer the following questions:*

*What was the situation? Was it a new situation for you to be in?*

_____
_____
_____
_____
_____

*Where were you? Was it in a new location?*

_____
_____
_____
_____
_____

*Who was with you? Were you with people you're familiar with or new acquaintances?*

_____
_____
_____
_____
_____

*What was happening? Was this a networking event, a training, a business meeting?*

_____

_____

_____

_____

_____

*What was being said?*

_____

_____

_____

_____

*How were you showing up?*

_____

_____

_____

_____

*How were others showing up around you?*

_____

_____

_____

_____

***

We covered a lot in this chapter on navigating your toxic stories. We talked about how easy it is to get lost in the toxic stories we tell ourselves, discussed common stories leaders tell themselves, and revisited the concept of confirmation bias. We also touched on why we have these stories and how they create negative impact in our lives, from our self-worth and self-esteem, to our personal relationships and our work performance. We discussed how to do your P.A.R.T. in navigating these toxic stories, by Pausing, Asking, Reflecting, and Taking Action to cast off old, toxic stories and develop healthier ones to replace them.

In the next and final chapter, we discuss how to overcome your toxic stories. We build upon the concepts we've learned throughout the book and discuss five ways in detail to help you overcome your toxic stories. We wrap up with some more journaling prompts to help you continue diving deep into your stories, even after you've finished working your way through this book.

# Chapter 5
# Overcome Our Toxic Stories

*"You may encounter many defeats, but you must not be defeated. In fact, it may be necessary to encounter the defeats, so you can know who you are, what you can rise from, how you can still come out of it."*

*- Maya Angelou, American poet, singer, memoirist, and civil rights activist*

I wish I could tell you, "Now that we know that these toxic stories exist, we'll be able to avoid them for the rest of our lives." But that's not the case (*and you definitely shouldn't expect that to happen!*).

What I *can* tell you is that you'll be more aware of them than ever before after reading this book and completing the Journal Prompts along the way. Awareness is the first and most important step toward growth and making a positive change in life.

Have you heard anyone say, "A person can only change when *she's* ready to change?" The emphasis is on the individual person making that decision. Others can want change for her, but only she holds the power to make real change happen in her life.

The same is true for each of us, whether in our personal lives, with our families and friends, or in our professional lives. Some of us are addicted to our toxic stories. We like to play the victim, to blame everyone else around us, and to wallow in our suffering and say, "Poor me" to anyone who will listen.

Why? Because it's far easier to continue living in and believing the toxic stories we hold, rather than do the deep inner work to uncover and overcome them. To face the fact that we aren't living up to our fullest potential. To create new, healthier stories that will help us create the kind of impact that both lights us on fire and terrifies us at the same time.

Only we have the power to make that change. Only we have the opportunity to say, "I will not believe this lie about myself today" and, instead, empower ourselves with stories that will help us reach our goals.

Is it easy? Hell no! Is it possible? Hell yes!

In this chapter, we explore six methods of overcoming toxic stories that I've found work best for my clients (and myself!) from my years of research and client work. We discuss each method and how to apply it, and I guide you through some final Journal Prompts to help you start taking action right away.

## Remember Your Worth

I started with the reminder to remember your worth because it's the most important method for overcoming toxic stories of them all. As we've discussed several times throughout the book, toxic stories have a tendency to strip us of our self-worth. It's critical to remember that we have value and worth in this world, regardless of what our gremlins are saying. Just because we might be struggling on our leadership journeys, in our professional careers generally, or in our personal lives, we are no less worthy of love, grace, and success.

So often, we associate our worth and value in this world with the promotions we receive, the growth we experience in our businesses, or the accolades we receive from those around us. None of these dictate your worth or your value. I'm writing this for you, because I'm also writing this for me.

It's easy to get wrapped up in the rat race of life—to compare ourselves to others in our industries, fields, and similar (or even different) family situations. This leads us to feel less than, incapable, or unworthy. This can hold us back from showing up fully in the world, reaching for our big goals, and creating the kind of impact we dream of having.

Don't allow yourself to get wrapped up in this dangerous game. The more you find yourself falling down the comparison trap, the more toxic stories you'll find yourself crafting and believing. And the harder it will be to get unstuck and create healthier stories.

When my clients are faced with their own toxic stories, I remind them to ask themselves: "Is this true about me?" If the client is really honest with herself, the answer is usually *no.* If she still feels like the answer is *yes,* then we brainstorm ways we can make the story false or find evidence to support the opposite of the toxic story. Let's take a look at a recurring story my client Kiara used to have and how we overcame it together using this method.

Kiara had been working in her highly successful product-based business by herself for a handful of years. When I first met Kiara, we talked about her business growth (or, rather, explosion!), and it was immediately evident to me that she needed to hire help. During the "slow" months in her business, she was working 16-hour days, six days per week. But when the holidays rolled around, Kiara was working nearly non-stop, around the clock, and getting about three hours of sleep at night. Needless to say, she was exhausted, precariously close to burnout, and feeling like she wanted to run away from the business she had built. When I asked her why she had waited so long to hire the help she needed, she replied, "I'm a behind-the-scenes person, not a leader."

I knew, as soon as the words slipped from her mouth, that this was a toxic story she was hanging on to—one that was holding her back from running a business she loved and living her life to the fullest. As we dug into her story, we uncovered a lot of fear around being in charge of someone other than herself. Kiara knew what needed to be done and she did it— *all*. But passing things off to someone else? That seemed too unnerving. A lot was going through Kiara's mind that many first-time leaders experience, like:

» *What if the person I hire is awful and I have to let her go?*
» *What if I have to tell my employee he's doing a bad job?*
» *What if I suck as a leader and my employees hate me?*
» *I can do things faster than trying to teach someone else how to do them.*
» *What will people think if I fail at this?*
» *Maybe I'm not good enough to be a leader.*

All of these fears and worries snowballed into one big toxic story in Kiara's mind: "I'm a behind-the-scenes person, not a leader." Just as we discussed in Chapter 2, Kiara had formed this toxic story as a barrier to protect herself. By being a "behind-the-scenes" person, she developed a toxic story that hid what was really going on in her mind, while creating a front that others readily understood and accepted. This toxic story kept her from hiring for much longer than she should have and until she simply couldn't avoid it any longer—unless she wanted to drastically reduced her business or, worse, close up shop.

When I first started working with Kiara, we started with this most important method for overcoming toxic stories: Remember your worth. Kiara was getting tied up in the failure aspect of hiring a team. Her self-worth was tangled up in a web of negative self-talk and worries. We worked through each excuse by asking this question: "Is this true?" And then we started replacing the worries with real examples, such as "Tell me about how you serve your customers." When Kiara told me how she goes above and beyond to communicate with customers, listen to their concerns and feedback, and shower them with fun surprises, I was able to turn this around and show her how she can leverage these skills with her team. She soon began to realize she could be a leader and actually enjoy the role. That she didn't have to become someone she wasn't in order to succeed. That she was enough and she was worthy of having the help she needed.

Does Kiara's story ring true for you, too? Or perhaps your own story is around feeling unworthy or less than in some regard. Take a few minutes and use the following Journal Prompt to remember your worth.

*Journal Prompt: Take some time to reflect on your positive qualities and experiences and remember your worth by using the following prompts. As a reminder, additional reader resources can be accessed at www.ashleycox.co/stories.*

*List 10 positive characteristics or qualities you possess.*

_____
_____
_____
_____
_____
_____

*List 10 things you do well in life or in business.*

_____

_____

_____

_____

_____

_____

*List 10 compliments you've received from others recently.*

_____

_____

_____

_____

_____

_____

## Journal Through Your Stories

Journaling is a great way to navigate and overcome your toxic stories. It helps us dig deep into the stories we're telling ourselves, to understand them and the roles they play in our lives, and to figure out the lessons we need to learn from those stories. Journaling helps us be open and honest with ourselves and move forward past the stories that aren't serving us well.

I love what Bukola Ogunwale, business coach and consultant at Bukola Ogunwale & Co., has to say about journaling on Goodreads: "Your journal is like your best friend. You don't have to pretend with it, you can be honest and write exactly how you feel." Her thoughts pair perfectly with what Christina Baldwin, writer and seminar presenter at PeerSpirit Inc., has to say, also on Goodreads: "Journal writing is a voyage to the interior."

If you're not into journaling, let me share some fun facts with you about the benefits journaling has on our physical, as well as our emotional, well-being. Studies have shown that the simple act of regular journaling can strengthen our immune cells, decrease the impact of chronic illnesses such as asthma and rheumatoid arthritis, and act as a stress-management tool to help us navigate stressful events.

Further scientific evidence supports that journaling has other unexpected benefits as well. According to the article "The Health Benefits of Journaling" (on the PsychCentral website), "The act of writing accesses your left brain, which is analytical and rational. While your left brain is occupied, your right brain is free to create, intuit and feel. Writing removes mental blocks and allows you to use all of your brainpower to better understand yourself, others and the world around you."

Among the benefits of journaling are:
- » Clarity of thoughts and feelings,
- » Knowing yourself better,
- » Stress reduction,
- » More effective problem-solving, and
- » Disagreement resolution.

Our journaling practice can be our own. Don't feel the need to journal every day or to write/fill 10 pages. Find what works and feels best for you. I prefer to spend just a few minutes each morning journaling. I start with jotting down a few things I'm grateful for, then practice some freewriting to work through any challenge(s) I might be dealing with, explore creative thoughts and ideas I have about my business, capture goals or dreams I have for my life, or note something funny or inspiring that happened the previous day. Some days I write more than other days. I occasionally skip a day or two (or even a week!) if I'm not feeling in the mood to journal. My journaling practice is perfectly imperfect, but it works for me. Find what works best for you.

When I'm struggling with my own toxic stories, I journal a lot more. If I'm dealing with something particularly challenging, I may even spend two to three hours journaling through what I'm worried about, the stories I'm telling myself, and the fears I'm struggling with. Journaling helps to clear all of the negativity and worry out of our bodies. Getting it all out of our heads and bodies and onto paper somehow makes the worries seem smaller and more insignificant—or, at the very least, it makes them feel more manageable.

Once we have everything out of our heads and onto paper, we can then ask ourselves whether these things are true about us or not, and whether or not they are serving us on our journey. We may even ask whether or not we need to take action on something.

Here are some helpful tips to get you started off on the right foot with journaling:

> » Start with a small goal. (For example, try journaling for two minutes a day for five consecutive days.)
> » Don't worry about spelling, punctuation, and grammar.
> » Allow your journaling to be a judgment-free zone. Nothing you write is good or bad.
> » Keep your journal secure, so you feel comfortable to write whatever you're feeling.

*Journal Prompt: If you're new to journaling, I recommend trying the five-day practice mentioned above before diving into this prompt. Think of it as a warm-up for a more strenuous exercise.*

*Once you're warmed up, or if you're an old pro, take 30 minutes to journal about a toxic story you're struggling with right now. Here are some questions you can answer for more clarity in tearing down your toxic story and crafting a new, healthier version for yourself:*

*What toxic story are you struggling with right now?*

_____
_____
_____
_____
_____


*Is this story true about you?*

» *If yes, why is is true and how can you transform the story so it becomes a healthy story?*

_____
_____
_____
_____
_____


*Why are you struggling with this story?*

_____
_____
_____
_____
_____


*Where did it come from?*

_____
_____

_____

_____

_____

*How would your life look different if you no longer had this toxic story?*

_____

_____

_____

_____

_____

_____

*How can you transform (or rewrite) this toxic story to be a healthy story instead? (Refer to the chart on page 103 in Chapter 3 for examples.)*

_____

_____

_____

_____

_____

*What is one step you can take today to move past this toxic story?*

_____

_____

_____

_____

_____

*What is one step you can take this month to create a new, healthier story?*

_____

_____

_____

_____

_____

*What will you do to celebrate when you've overcome this toxic story?*

_____

_____

_____

_____

Another strategy that's worked really well for me is a daily gratitude practice, which I mentioned briefly above. This doesn't have to be fancy or overly complicated. I like to combine my gratitude and daily journaling in the same practice. I keep a small notebook on my desk, and each morning I jot down three to five things I'm grateful for before doing a few minutes of freewriting before I start my day. It's a simple but very effective way to start your day off on the right foot and retrain your brain to develop positive and grateful stories throughout the day (versus finding yourself stuck in the victim cycle).

## Meditate or Practice Yoga

When I'm feeling particularly stuck in my head or emotions, I enjoy a brief meditation or yoga practice to help me overcome my toxic stories. (There are many guided meditations available through podcast platforms and great yoga videos on YouTube.)

You might be rolling your eyes at me while reading this. I get it. I used to think it was a bunch of fluff—until I gave it a try. You don't have to be a super woo-woo person to appreciate and reap the benefits of meditation and yoga. Several scientific studies over the years have consistently shown that people who regularly mediate have overall better wellness, reduced anxiety, less stress (and less of the stress-related hormone cortisol), significantly reduced chances for heart attacks, strokes, and even cancer, as well as being more self-confident, more productive, happier, and more independent. In addition, those who practice yoga on a consistent basis see many of the same benefits mentioned previously, plus relief for joint and body pain, reduced weight, and improved quality of life.

What's not to love about all those great benefits?!

It's better to work through our emotions and thoughts than try to suppress or ignore them altogether. We spend far more time and energy trying to cram them all down and forget about them than we do working through them.

Meditation and yoga can help us not only live healthier lives, but also bring a great deal of clarity and calmness around whatever we might be facing.

Have you ever tried really hard to remember something you've forgotten and then, as soon as you changed tasks/ started working on something else, it came so easily to you?

Meditation and yoga can do the same when we're stuck in a particular toxic story. Once we step away from the story we've been telling ourselves and focus on something else, we can look at the situation more objectively and determine whether it's true or not. Yoga and meditation can both help us step away from what we're dealing with, work through the emotions and thoughts racing through our minds, and approach the situation with more clarity, ease, and confidence.

When we're able to look at a situation more objectively, then we're able to release toxic stories that aren't serving us and fill that space with healthy stories that support our dreams and goals. This next Journal Prompt will help you get started with some simple meditation and yoga practices.

*Journal Prompt*: *Try the following simple practices to experience the benefits of meditation and/or yoga:*

» Meditation: Set a timer on your phone for five minutes. Sit or lie down in a comfortable position with your eyes closed. (Don't feel the need to sit cross-legged or with your hands in any particular position. Just get comfortable!) Focus on your breathing. As you sit quietly, your mind will wander. When you notice it wandering, bring your focus back to your breath. Once you've completed your five-minute meditation, journal through anything that came up for you during your quiet time. (This is usually when the most clarity comes for me about something I've been struggling with, but it may take a few sessions to ease into your practice and get those aha moments.)

» Yoga: You don't not need to be an expert yogi to gain the benefits of yoga! Search "beginner's yoga" on YouTube and try a simple stretching practice that is only 10 minutes long. My favorite online instructor is Yoga with Adriene. She's super down to earth, her style is very approachable, and she has a lot of great beginner options.

## Remove Yourself from Toxic Situations

Next, let's discuss an often-tricky method for overcoming toxic stories, which is to remove yourself from toxic situations. A quick disclaimer for this method: This tactic may or may not work for you, depending on your situation. However, that doesn't mean I'm giving you permission to skip right over this method. I still challenge you to consider this as an option, even though it may not seem like the most logical choice at first glance.

Throughout this book, we have discussed how we (humans) have a tendency to get wrapped up in confirmation bias. We find ourselves looking for evidence to support a toxic story. We often find it easier to believe the story we've created, rather than see the truth of the situation.

That's why it's important to look around and see if the environment we're in is feeding a toxic story we're holding onto—and if it is, to remove ourselves from that situation. But what does it look like when a situation or the people around us are supporting a toxic story in our lives?

A situation that supports a toxic story might be one that doesn't allow us to try new things, create new experiences, or change the way we're showing up in the world. It can feel stifling and even downright suffocating. We may feel trapped, stagnant, and hopeless. The situation may be an awful job we despise, the town we live in, or even the car we drive. These situations become cages that hold us back from reaching our full potential.

The people we surround ourselves with on a daily basis can have a similar impact. They may mirror our own toxic stories and perpetuate the stories and untruths we tell ourselves. They may even be drowning in their own unique toxic stories and pulling us down into a victim cycle. When we see those stories reflected in the ones we surround ourselves with, we can easily believe that our problem has to be something happening *to* us (as opposed to remembering that we have the power to change what's going on around us). These people can be our spouses or partners, family members, and even friends. This can even happen through social media. I bet you can easily name that one person who always seems to be complaining and blaming everyone around them for their sufferings.

You may not be able to upend your whole life and start fresh, but it's worth evaluating your circumstances and determining what you can change (like finding a new job) versus what you need to learn to navigate more effectively (like your strained relationship with your mom).

The more we find ourselves in toxic situations or surrounded by people with perpetual toxic stories, the further we sink into the quicksand of toxic stories and the harder it is for us to break free.

*Journal Prompt: Unsure of whether or not you need to remove yourself from a toxic situation or part ways with a toxic person? Ask yourself the following questions to see if a change of scenery might do you good.*

*Is the situation I'm in supporting the toxic story I've been telling myself?*

_____

_____

_____

_____

_____

*Are the people I'm associating with supporting the toxic story I've been telling myself?*

_____

_____

_____

_____

_____

*Are there opportunities for me to develop a new, healthier story in this space?*

_____

_____

_____

_____

_____

*Is there an opportunity for me to change my situation?*

_____

_____

_____

_____

*Is there an opportunity for me to part ways with toxic people in my life?*

_____

_____

_____

_____

*How can I connect with different people who can help support a healthier story?*

_____

_____

_____

_____

# Lean on a Trusted Confidant

In life and in leadership, the road can get rough and worn. Sometimes, it can feel like we're treading the same path over and over again. Other times, it feels as though we've stumbled onto some unknown trail far from all that is familiar and safe.

There will be good times and there will be struggles. There will times of pure joy, achievement, and success. And there will be times of seemingly insurmountable challenges and defeat.

Through all of these times, it's important to have someone we can trust on standby to help us overcome our toxic stories. The person we can text or call. The one who'll meet us for coffee at the drop of a hat. The confidant we can share our fears and insecurities with and who will listen without judgment, offer advice, and give us a reality check when we need one.

I've found on my journey that the act of simply talking through whatever I'm dealing with is a great way to help me process my feelings and what's happening in my brain. It's absolutely essential to me as a business owner to have friends, mentors, coaches, and advisors who are also business owners (as they truly understand the emotional roller coaster that this journey is) and have their own toxic stories that they've dealt with. It's also important to have friends and trusted mentors to help you through life's everyday challenges outside of your professional life.

*Journal Prompt: Before you find yourself dealing with toxic thoughts about your ability to lead, identify a confidant who can help you work through them when the time comes. Then, provide them with this guide to help guide the conversation when the time comes:*

*What are you worrying the most about right now?*

_____

_____

_____

_____

_____

*Is this thought/worry/story helpful?*

_____

_____

_____

_____

_____

*Where did this thought/worry/story stem from?*

_____

_____

_____

_____

_____

*Can you remove yourself from the situation and/or people who are feeding this worry?*

_____

_____

_____

_____

_____

*How do you see this working out for the best in the end?*

_____

_____

_____

_____

_____

*What is one action you can take right now to move forward?*

_____

_____

_____

_____

_____

Yes, we could each walk through these questions on our own. But it's far more effective to have a neutral party helping us work through challenging situations, to hold space for us to feel big emotions, to work through toxic stories that are holding us back, and to gently push us along when we're holding back.

Take a few minutes right now to prepare yourself and your confidant so you'll both be ready if and when the next rough day hits.

## Give Yourself Space

I don't believe in making excuses or wallowing in self-pity, but I also don't believe in pushing down real thoughts, real fears, and real emotions. Some days are more productive than others and you crush your to-do list; others are more challenging and require a different pace.

I truly believe we ebb and flow in life and business. We have seasons when we're riding high and feeling like a champion, and others when it feels like the wave we were just riding crashed down on top of us and we're drowning.

In those times when we're feeling the weight of that wave and the suffocation of the water around us, it's okay to step back and give ourselves some space. There are times in our journeys when nothing is going to help except space.

In this space, we learn about ourselves in ways we might not otherwise. But we have to make wise use of this time so we don't find ourselves wallowing in self-pity and falling further and further down the hole of our toxic stories. The following Journal Prompt contains some strategies you can use to make sure the space you're taking is intentional and helpful.

*Journal Prompt: When your toxic stories are weighing heavy on you and you need some space, set an intention around why you're taking space, define how long you will take space (an hour, a half-day, a full-day, etc.), and then try one (or more) of these strategies.*

» Take a mental health day.
» Read a fictional book.
» Dance to music.
» Draw, paint, or color.
» Watch a funny show on Netflix.
» Call someone you love.
» Sit outside and enjoy nature.
» Go for a walk at a park (bonus points if you take your pup along!).

Above all, remember that we are worth so much more than the hurtful, toxic stories we've been telling ourselves. We each have so much to give in this world, and this world is a better place simply for us being here.

\*\*\*

We covered just a handful of my favorite ways to work through toxic stories in this chapter. Based on my work coaching and mentoring women over the years, as well as researching this topic, these are the six things that I've found work best for my clients and myself. There are many more ways to overcome toxic stories in your life, however, and I encourage you to find what works for you. (I'd love to hear from you to learn what you've found that works best! Reach out to me at mystory@ashleycox.co to share your journey and tell me how you've overcome your own toxic stories.)

# Final Thoughts

*"Step out of the history that is holding you back. Step into the new story you are willing to create."*

- Oprah Winfrey

We've been on quite a journey together, friend. Thank you for coming along with me to explore the concept of toxic stories we tell ourselves that hold us back from reaching our full potential. My hope is that you feel more confident as a leader now—that you're able to identify your toxic stories and navigate them successfully to be the leader you were born to be and to create the impact you desire to have in this world.

We've discussed what stories are, clarified the differences between healthy stories and toxic ones, and uncovered who has toxic stories. *(Reminder: We all experience them!)* We've discussed where these toxic stories come from and how we form new ones.

We've talked about the important role that stories play in our lives and how, when left unchecked, they can have significant negative impacts on our self-esteem, self-worth, health, and mental well-being, not to mention our relationships and our professional journeys.

Finally, we learned how to navigate these toxic stories and overcome them so that we can live a more productive, happier, and more intentional life—and the reason you're probably reading this book: so that we can step into our leadership roles with more confidence and courage, to reach our full potential and have greater impact in the world.

A prevalent and very toxic narrative I held early on in my business journey was "I don't know anything about starting and running a business." It's not an uncommon story to have. It might manifest in different ways for different people, but it often sounds like this:

> » "I have no idea where to even start."
> » "I don't know anything about taxes. I could never figure them out!"
> » "What if no one wants what I'm selling?"
> » "I'll never figure this out and it's going to be such a waste of time and money."

Sure, there are going to be things you don't know if you're starting a business. It's a pretty big undertaking. There are also many things you don't know if you work in the corporate world and take on a new position. But along the way, you learn the things you need to know. You get training and practice new skills and become proficient in a job you once knew very little or nothing about.

Too often, we automatically think we're failures because we weren't born with the immediate knowledge, skills, or expertise that would make our lives easier. (Wouldn't that be nice?)

Remember that doctors, professional athletes, and world-renowned musicians have spent years—even decades—of their lives dedicated to their crafts and professions. They didn't wake up one morning and just "know" how to perform surgery, throw a perfect touchdown pass, or flawlessly perform Mozart's "Eine Kleine Nachtmusik."

They studied, received training, practiced, worked with mentors and advisors, practiced some more, made mistakes, received critiques, and, yes, practiced some more. (Obviously, there are always exceptions to the rule, but generally speaking, these anomalies don't happen for the great majority of us.) Had they given up before they even got started, imagine what the world would be missing today.

## The Choice Is Yours

The good news is, we have a choice:

> Choose to live in the toxic stories we've created.
> *or*
> Choose to change our story.

When we choose to believe the lies we tell ourselves about why we can't do something or be the person we wish to be, and revel in playing the victim, we can allow ourselves to get stuck in the toxic story cycle: We have an experience we perceive as bad, create a toxic story around it, and look for evidence (confirmation bias) that supports the story as being true.

Have you ever heard the saying *Negativity breeds negativity*? It's definitely true in this case. The more we feel sorry for ourselves, the more we place the blame on someone or something else, the more we make the decision to believe and stay in the toxic stories we tell ourselves, the more we will.

However, when we choose to look internally and take ownership of our story, only then will we be able to make a positive change. Because just as negativity breeds negativity, the same is true for positivity. And just as a reminder, it's okay to be in the emotions that don't feel so good, as long as you don't allow yourself to stay in them indefinitely.

We each get to craft our own story. Just as I'm creating and writing this book—these very words— you too can write the book of your own story. You get to consciously write your story each and every day, with the thoughts you think, the words you say, the actions you take, and the people you spend time with.

We can choose to get stuck in the quicksand of our thoughts, or use them to create a strong foundation on which to build our tower.

When it comes to leadership, we have to build our own foundation before we can add team members to help us construct the tower. Without a strong foundation as a leader, we don't have anything to build upon. No, I don't mean that we have to build a powerhouse of a business alone before adding team members. We need a mentally strong foundation.

Think about it this way.

Say a contractor is building a house. The contractor digs out the earth and pours concrete to build the foundation. But the contractor does a poor job of pouring the concrete. It's full of air pockets and unlevel. When the contractor brings in a team to help build the house, do you think the house will have a strong foundation upon which to stand? Of course not! No matter how well-built the house is, it will not last on a foundation that's unstable.

The same is true for us. When we try to lead teams without having a strong foundation in place, it's a recipe for struggle, overwhelm, and, eventually, demise.

Our foundations as leaders are the stories we tell and believe about ourselves and our abilities. If we constantly tell ourselves that we're not cut out to be leaders, guess what? We won't be good leaders. We'll know it, our teams will know it, and even our customers will likely know it. Things will start to fall through the cracks, quality will suffer, customer service will wane, progress will stifle, and so forth. Our leadership impacts every other single aspect of business.

Being a great leader starts with having the right mindset—telling ourselves the truth and challenging the toxic stories that pop up in our minds. This doesn't mean we have to lie to ourselves! We simply need to be aware that every thought crossing our minds may not be the truth and, through self-awareness and personal responsibility, take the actions that we need to challenge those assumptions and replace the toxic stories with truths.

Remember to ask, "Is this true about me?" Or are fear, worry, and self-doubt creeping in? Here's a quick exercise to use any time a toxic story pops up. Try this right now with something that's been nagging at the back of your mind.

### *Journal Prompt:*

*As a reminder, additional reader resources can be accessed at www.ashleycox.co/stories.*

*Write down the toxic story you've been telling yourself, exactly as it pops up in your mind.*

_____

_____

_____

_____

*Now, dissect each part of this story and ask yourself, "Is this true?"*

_____

_____

_____

_____

*For any of the sections you feel are true, ask yourself, "Why is this true about me?"*

_____

_____

_____

_____

*Now ask yourself, "What can I do to improve in this area?" (Get really specific here!)*

_____

_____

_____

_____

Commit to making this improvement by writing it down along with a deadline for making it happen.

I will commit to _____

_____ by _____.

This is a quick, easy exercise that you can do anywhere and at any time. By doing this exercise, you'll quickly be able to identify that most of what you're telling yourself is false and not founded on anything substantial. It's simply fear creeping in and taking over. But for those areas in which there is truth, you'll be able to take a more objective look at the situation and create a plan for how to improve and move forward in that area to become a more confident and impactful leader.

Every toxic story you have will not be true, but some will be. A story is only negative when either a) it's untrue, or b) you obsessively think about it.

If it's untrue, let it go.

If it's true, then stop obsessing and take action.

Taking action is the only way to overcome that toxic story, to change our story for the better, to become the leader we desire to be, and to cast off the chains of uncertainty, fear, and doubt.

But we can't just do this once and think all our stories will be changed for good from now until the end of time. Unfortunately, that's not how it works.

With each new step in our journey, new stories will pop

up. As we learn, grow, and overcome old ones, new ones will wriggle their way into the spaces left behind by the old. Our mind's job is to solve problems. However, when it doesn't have a worthy problem to solve, it likes to create new ones to keep itself busy. Backward, I know, but once we know this, we can be more in tune with what's going on in the moment and navigate those budding toxic stories before they become bigger problems to deal with later.

Clearing out our toxic stories is a process, an ongoing activity, or a practice, if you will. When we begin to recognize that we're slipping into a false story about our abilities or our situation, we simply go through this exercise to clear out those damaging stories and take meaningful and positive action steps to improve in those areas and create new, healthier stories for which to live by.

As we get started, those toxic stories might not be as easy to identify. They creep in slowly and stealthily, like thieves in the night. They slip into our dreams and our thoughts when we least expect them. Most of the time, they pop up when we're not even doing something related to the thought. They can quickly induce a quickened heartbeat, clammy palms, and a sweaty brow. We start to feel anxious and overwhelmed by "But what if this is true?!" feelings. Things can quickly spiral out of control until we're questioning anything and everything we've ever done as a human being. Whew—that got real, quick!

As we get more familiar with recognizing our own spiraling stories, we'll be able to get ahead of them and stop them before things get too out of control. The goal isn't to stop these toxic stories. That's an unrealistic goal. The human brain was designed to help us avoid danger and solve problems. Thankfully, it does its job pretty well. It's why we don't go flinging ourselves off of cliffs or putting our hands into roaring fires.

But it's also why leading a team both is exciting and scares the shit out of us. Our brains are firing on all synapses and thinking of all the ways this could go horribly wrong. Like . . .

» *What if this is really hard?*
» *What if having a team means I have to work even more hours?*
» *What if I no good at giving directions?*
» *What if I hire the wrong person and I have to fire them?*
» *What if my employee steals from me?*
» *What if they don't do the work the same way I do?*
» *What if my customer service suffers and my business fails?*
» *What if I lose everything I've worked so hard for to this point?*
» *What if I have to talk to an employee about something uncomfortable?*
» *What if my employee doesn't do their job correctly?*
» *What if I really don't know what I'm doing at all?*

What if, what if, what if.

*What if* is not a predictor of the future. It's simply our brains running through the list of *all* the possible ways a situation could go horribly wrong. That doesn't mean they will come true. It doesn't mean we're horrible leaders. It doesn't mean that this isn't the right next step to take in our businesses.

It may mean there are opportunities for us to learn and grow. It may mean there are things to watch out for in order to avoid bigger problems. It may mean a lot of things.

But it doesn't mean we should curl up in a ball, avoid everyone and everything, and stop living life or growing our business or moving up the corporate ladder.

Just like it was scary as hell to start our own businesses, or advance in our careers, we figured it out—and we will also figure out this leadership journey.

***Journal Prompt****: Think of all the ways that you successfully overcame the toxic stories you had when you started your business or received your first promotion. List those here:*

*(Examples: watched a free webinar, signed up for a course, talked to a business friend, got a mentor)*

_____

_____

_____

_____

_____

_____

*Now, think of ways you can overcome these toxic stories about becoming or being a leader. List those here:*

*(Examples: read a book on leadership (wink), talked to an experienced leader about their journey, read biographies from famous leaders about their struggles)*

_____

_____

_____

_____

_____

_____

By taking some time to reflect and journal about what's going through your mind, you'll be able to step back, take an objective look at what's really going on, and then create a plan for overcoming those fears, doubts, and worries that you're not going to be as great of a leader as you desire to be.

I also recommend getting a friend or mentor to support us on this journey, someone who will openly and honestly share where they feel we're succumbing to a toxic story and where they see opportunities for improvement. Not every story we tell ourselves will be true. But not every story we tell ourselves will be false, either. Knowing the difference between the two, and taking action on those that are true in order to grow and become a stronger leader, are important. A friend or mentor who knows us well and is willing to help provide an outside perspective will be a great resource on our leadership journey.

## Change Your Story, Change Your Life

I hope that through the pages of this book, you've been able to go on your own expedition to uncover the thoughts and stories holding you back from achieving your full potential and your greatest life's purpose—the reason you are here on this earth.

When you choose to change your story, you choose to change your life. You are more than capable and equipped to take the action that you need in order to reach your fullest potential.

Now that we've reached the end of this journey together, I encourage you to find a mentor or advisor to support you in your leadership goals. Dig deep and do the inner work, friend. You can become a confident and courageous leader, if you're willing to stop believing the toxic stories you hold and create stronger, more empowering, and healthy stories in their place.

I invite you to connect with me on social media or email me directly at mystory@ashleycox.co. I love to connect with my readers and followers to hear how you have broken through toxic stories, overcome challenges to become a confident and courageous leader, and impacted the world.

# *Appendix*

# **Transform Our Toxic Team Stories**

Transforming our own stories is the most important area to focus on in our leadership journey. That's why the book you're reading starts with you. Many leaders I've worked with throughout the years start with their team first. They believe (most of the time subconsciously) that if they "fix" their team members, then they will naturally become better leaders. Unfortunately, that's not how it works. You can't fix other people to become a better leader. You can't rely on hiring a team of "A players" to solve all your problems. If you don't know how to lead "A players," they won't stay around for long. If you're not willing to start with yourself first, you might not be ready to lead a team.

Without our own healthy stories in place, it's impossible to help anyone else. Think about the safety announcements flight attendants make before an aircraft takes off. They remind us that in case of emergency, we should put on our own oxygen masks before helping those sitting near us. The logic is that if we can't breathe, we can't help anyone else breathe either.

The same is true when leading teams. If we are living with our own toxic stories about our ability to lead, we will not be well-prepared to help our team members succeed. We'll be gasping for air while trying to help them—and fighting a losing battle the whole time.

I strongly urge you before you start thinking about your team's needs to consider your own first. A great place to begin is within the pages of this book. Use the concepts and Journal Prompts to overcome your own toxic stories (aka put on your oxygen mask) before trying to help those around you.

When you've started making progress, you can then begin to reach out to help your team members, which is why I wanted to include a section about transforming our team stories. Often, just like we have toxic stories about ourselves, we carry around toxic stories about our teams. We need to reframe these stories in order to empower ourselves and our teams to reach greater success together.

The process for transforming the toxic stories we hold about our teams is very similar to the process for transforming our own stories that we've discussed throughout this book. It's about self-exploration and uncovering why we feel and think the way we do about our teams. It's about reflecting, asking questions, and digging deeper into the why behind the toxic story.

Following are three examples of stories I hear most frequently from leaders about their teams. You might find that you have the same or similar stories about your own team. With each example, I walk you through several questions you can use to learn more about why you might be forming these toxic stories about your team. Use these questions to test your assumptions and work toward overcoming them.

As you read through the stories and corresponding questions, you'll see a pattern for the types of questions you can ask about your team. You can use a similar vein of questions for any type of stories you have that are holding you and your team back from reaching your full potential together.

***"I have the worst team. I hired all the wrong people."***

> » Is my whole team "the worst?" Or is it really one or two people who are causing most of the issues?
> » If my team is underperforming, where are they underperforming and why?
> » How can I help my team in a way I haven't tried before?
> » Have I communicated the expectations to them clearly and frequently?
> » Does one or more of my team members need some additional training?
> » Have I shared the company vision and goals with them?
> » Do I have the right people in the right jobs doing the right tasks?

***"My team never follows through."***

> » Am I giving my team enough direction?
> » Does each team member fully understand their role?
> » Do I set clear enough deadlines, follow up with my team members along the way, and stick to the deadlines?
> » Am I checking in with my team frequently to see if there are any roadblocks I can help them remove?
> » Do we have clear processes in place for our work so that everyone is informed and involved at the right times during each project?
> » Are there any communication gaps in our workflow processes?
> » Do any of my team members need additional training or support in order to do their best work?

***"My team isn't as motivated as I need them to be."***

» Is the whole team unmotivated or just one person?

» What's the root cause of the lack of motivation? (This will require talking with your team members and asking them what's going on in their world. The key here is open and honest communication without judgment or negative repercussions.)

» What things truly motivate my team (positive reinforcement, flextime, small gifts/treats, etc.)?

» Am I sharing an inspiring vision for the future the whole team can get excited about?

» Have I set clear, specific, and measurable goals for my team that align with the company vision and goals?

» Am I checking in with my team members regularly and frequently to talk about their progress?

» Do I seek my team's feedback and use their ideas to help us improve together?

Now that you've read through these toxic story examples and prompt questions, here's a helpful tip: Consider this process like a scientist. Your toxic stories are assumptions, or hypotheses, that you want to test. The questions outlined here will help you probe deeper into what is true and false about your situation. As you answer the questions, try to remain as objective as possible. You might find some of the issues with your team stem from something you may or may not be doing. That's okay. We are all human. We aren't born with all the skills we need to be highly effective leaders. Just like everything else in life, leadership is a skill we must learn, practice, and develop over time in order to become proficient. Be open-minded and consider all the possibilities why your team isn't performing up to your expectations—even if the reason might be you.

Holding onto toxic stories about your team is detrimental to your business. Wherever these stories stemmed from, they cause us to form assumptions and beliefs about our teams. The more we tell ourself that our team is awful, the more likely we are to believe it. Remember when we discussed confirmation bias in Chapter 1? We further confirm our bias by looking for evidence that supports our beliefs, often subconsciously. Then, without even realizing it, our words, behaviors, and actions begin to mirror those beliefs. Our team members sense the subtle cues we are giving and respond accordingly. We have the power to influence the success, or failure, of our teams simply by how we interact with them. That is an incredible amount of power—a massive responsibility—and one that shouldn't be taken lightly.

There is a psychological phenomenon called the Pygmalion effect "wherein high expectations lead to improved performance in a given area" (according to the website Farnham Street). I often add that people will also perform down to our lowest expectations of them. Essentially, when we expect someone to succeed, we treat them one way; when we expect them to fail, we treat them a completely different way. Without even realizing it, our behaviors, actions, and words can greatly impact other people's performance. When we are aware of this, we can create a team of high performers; when we are not aware of this effect, the opposite can be true. I encourage you to consider the stories and assumptions you hold about your team and objectively look at the way in which you're treating each team member by using the following Journal Prompt.

*What are some toxic stories you currently have about your team?*

_____

_____

_____

_____

_____

*What questions from the examples above can you ask to probe deeper into the root cause of these toxic stories?*

_____

_____

_____

_____

_____

*What are three steps you can take right now to start overcoming these toxic stories and helping your team succeed?*

_____

_____

_____

_____

_____

As you dig into the specific issues you're facing with your team and begin diagnosing the root cause of your issues, you'll be able to craft a much more thoughtful and successful plan for how to handle the situation now and in the future. You'll start seeing major improvements in the way your team functions, responds, works together, and performs overall.

# A Grateful Heart

I had no idea what I was getting myself into when I decided to write a book. It's a . . . *process* . . . to say the least! However, from the time I was a young girl growing up in rural southern West Virginia, I knew I would write a book one day. Writing was always a major part of my life, from songs and short stories to poems and plays (some of which were very good, while others are a bit more embarrassing to stumble across). What I wasn't prepared for, though, was how challenging this process would be. I've always been a gifted writer, so I naively thought, *"Writing a book—piece of cake!"* But this process stretched me and helped me grow in ways I didn't even know I needed, and allowed me to share my stories, experiences, and lessons learned in a way I have never been able to do before. With that said, the fact that you're holding this book in your hands right now (whether in physical or electronic form) is one of my greatest life's achievements (so far!). And it wouldn't be in existence if it wasn't for several incredible people who have been by my side throughout my life and throughout this process. It's with a truly humble and grateful heart that I recognize and thank those people.

To my momma, Diana Walker: The woman who gave me life, always believed in me, and helped me grow up to become the woman I am today. Thank you from the bottom of my heart and the depths of my soul. You are my role model and the kind of woman I aspire to be. I love you.

To my husband, Mike Cox: You are the one who unwaveringly stands by my side, never bats an eyelash when I dream up some new adventure to embark upon, and can always be counted on to cheer me up, even on the hardest of days. I can truthfully say that I don't know what I would do or where I would be without you. I love you.

To my sister, Sara Foster, and brother, Troy Walker: Life is such a grand adventure and I'm beyond grateful that I have both of you by my side to enjoy it with. Being the oldest sibling comes with a lot of pressure; you're born a leader whether you want to be or not. I truly hope I've done you proud. I love you both.

To my extended family and family-in-love (aka in-laws): Thank you for always being there, cheering me on, loving me through the hard times, and believing in me. Family is one of the most amazing gifts to have as a human—and I'm incredibly blessed that you are mine. I love you all.

To my friends: If we talk regularly, if you've known about this book-writing process since the beginning, if you've helped me along the way, if you know you could call on me and I'd drop everything to be there for you, then I'm talking to and thinking of you as I write this note of gratitude. Thank you for your endless support, encouragement, kind words, and grace. Thank you for making me laugh, lending your shoulder for me to cry on, and loving me unconditionally in life and in business.

To my book designer, Jessica Freeman: The way you just get me is uncanny. To knock it out of the park with the cover design in less than 24 hours blew me away. I remember thinking, *"It wasn't that easy, was it?!"* Thank you for being so organized, intuitive, and a pleasure to work with. You made the book design process simple, approachable, and fun! I so appreciate you and all the work you did behind the scenes to make this book (and dream!) literally come to life in the form of real pages that people can hold in their hands.

To my book-writing coach and editor, Jodi Brandon: I'm not sure where to start, my friend. Whenever I read other authors' acknowledgment sections, I always wondered why so much credit was given to the editor—but now I know. I can truly say, with every fiber of my being, that this book would literally not exist without you. And if, by some chance miracle, it did, it wouldn't be a fraction as good as it is. Thank you for your guidance, your tough love, your encouragement, your advice, your mentorship, your emotional support, your friendship, your professionalism, your expertise, and your willingness to guide me through this incredible process from start to finish with endless amounts of grace and patience. I now understand the depth of respect, admiration, and love my fellow authors speak about in the pages of their own acknowledgments. Thank you with my deepest gratitude.

To my beta readers: Thank you for being my guinea pigs—seriously! I know my book was a hot mess when you first got your eyeballs on it. And I'm so grateful that you stuck it out and read through the messy beginning to help me refine, edit, expand, and further develop the content within the pages of this book. You truly helped me create the most impact possible with your help and support.

To each of you mentioned here: We did it. We did it! WE WROTE A BOOK!! I hope you take the time to celebrate this accomplishment along with me, because without you, it wouldn't have come to pass. Cheers to book #1 being, well, in the books!

Finally, to you, the reader. Thank you for picking up this book, reading these words, journaling your heart out, and overcoming your toxic stories alongside me. Remember, you are so much more capable than you know.

# About the Author

Ashley Cox, PHR, SHRM-CP is a leadership mentor for women. She graduated from Concord University with her bachelor's degree in business administration with concentrations in management and marketing, and worked in leadership positions and human resources with Kroger and J.Crew for several years before starting her own business in 2015.

Ashley's biggest passion is helping women tap into and leverage their natural strengths in order to lead in a way that feels good and gets results. She fully believes that the world needs more of the unique qualities and characteristics that women bring to leadership positions—and she's on a mission to help them do just that.

As an active member in her local community, Ashley loves to give back by serving as a member on the Junior Board of Directors for the YWCA of Northeast Tennessee and Southwest Virginia and on the Board of Directors for Dare 2 Be You Recovery. She was chosen as a 40 Under Forty recipient by the *Tri-Cities Business Journal* in 2017 and recognized as one of the Rising Tide Society and Honeybook's 20 On the Rise recipients in 2018.

Raised in West Virginia, Ashley is proud of her Appalachian heritage and the beautiful state she calls home. She grew up exploring the forests and streams barefoot, soaking in the sunshine and sweet mountain air, and dreaming of how she hoped to change the world one day. She currently resides with her husband, Mike, in East Tennessee, where they enjoy going on grand adventures, spending lazy days kayaking local rivers, and hanging around the house working on projects together. In the mornings, you will find Ashley sipping her coffee on the back porch with her beloved border collie-hound rescue dog, Myla, and snuggling with her family on the couch by night.

Connect with Ashley on Instagram @ashleycox.co, where she shares education and inspiration for women leaders, snippets of her life and adventures, and behind-the-scenes glimpses of how it all goes down.

Visit www.ashleycox.co to learn more about Ashley and her work with women in leadership.